Moving IN Close

Moving IN Close

52 BIBLE STUDY TIPS
TO HELP YOU KNOW GOD

CHRISTY FITZWATER

ISBN 9781092498432 (paperback)

Table of Contents

INTRODUCTION

I grew up in church and loved the Bible, but I didn't have skills for studying it until I was in my early thirties. Then one day I signed up for a new Bible study class at church, taught by a brilliant woman with a sophisticated haircut. Expecting to walk in and soak up Bible truth, I was shocked when she started teaching us method instead. What was this?

As we marked the Scriptures and made lists and charts, it felt very much like college, and I loved the fact that I was the one being asked to pick up the shovel and do all of the work of studying. Because I had this idea that only a gifted few, like preachers and Beth Moore, could really figure out such a complex book as the Bible, I had been dependent on others. Now I was learning how to discover truth for myself.

Gaining the skills to understand God's word independently transformed my relationship with him. I began to understand and relate to him in a rich way, and I started to discover new truths, as if I were opening the Bible for the first time. I want you to have that same experience.

The Bible is a thick, complicated compilation of literature, and I've known so many people who have expressed their frustration with understanding it. It seems daunting even to know where to open and begin. May I offer that when it comes to giving do-able tips for studying the Bible, I'm your huckleberry?

"I'm your huckleberry" is an old expression we use often here in Kalispell, Montana, because huckleberries grow wild on the sides of our mountains. (Come visit me, and I'll buy you some huckleberry syrup as a souvenir.) To be your huckleberry means "I'm the one you're looking for; I'm the man for the job."

Since I have a degree in English, this word stuff comes easily to me. I'm also used to breaking down the Bible so that kids can understand it. Every Wednesday night at church, I stand in front of fifty or so grade school kids and teach them a lesson on their memory verse for the week. Just this last week, I demonstrated the basics of studying the Bible, then asked, "Don't you think you are capable, at your age, to do these things?" They said yes!

Adults often need things to be made that clear and simple, too. So let me talk to you about how to study the Bible, and by the end of these fifty-two different tips, I think you might be sitting back and breathing a bit. You might even say, "Okay, maybe I can understand the Bible after all."

But let's aim for more than that. I want my children at church to know God – to understand who he is and to enjoy a close relationship with him. It's what I want for you, too. This big, intimidating book, the Bible, is your key to intimacy with the God who loves you. So enjoy it. God is using his words to draw you to himself.

BIBLE STUDY TIP #1

Let your motive be relationship with God.

My first counsel to you is that you always, always, always read the Bible with relationship in mind. This is not a textbook. It's not a chore on your list. It's a compilation of words, tucked into a leather binding, from a very kind and loving WHO. This book is filled with words you need *today*, from a God who sees exactly what you're going through and what you need in all the deep corners of your heart. I don't think you can imagine how badly God wants you to know him and to experience all that he has for you in your everyday life.

Read Jeremiah 9:23-24 (one of my faaaaavorites):

> *This is what the LORD says: "Let not the wise boast of their wisdom or the strong boast of their strength or the rich boast of their riches, but let the one who boasts boast about this: that they have the understanding to know me,*

that I am the LORD, who exercises kindness,
justice and righteousness on earth, for in these
I delight," declares the LORD.

Now may I suggest that you find a notebook that you can keep handy as you work through these Bible study tips? Take your time answering the following questions:

1. In this passage, WHO has a relationship with WHOM?
2. According to this verse, is it an option for you to have a relationship with the LORD?
3. If this were the only verse you had ever read from the Bible, how would you feel about having a relationship with this "LORD"?

Before you really dig into the Bible, you have to secure your hope that God is not aloof and unapproachable, that he wants to be known, and that your searching will be rewarded with finding.

BIBLE STUDY TIP #2

Ask God to show you wonderful things in his law.

"Look at all of those scuds!" he said.

I'm a woman working on her third language, but I still didn't know what in the world my husband was talking about. He pointed to where the frigid lake water touched the rocky shore, and we squatted down. "See that?" he said, pointing to a four-millimeter-long fish kind of thing swimming in the water. (Was it some kind of freshwater shrimp? I don't know. I tried Google but only came up with 147 videos about how to tie the fly.)

I was enjoying our Sunday trip to Rogers Lake, as only Montana folks can enjoy a beautiful spring day after months of winter. Hearing the birds, smelling the pine, and seeing the ice diminishing on the lake brought hope to my soul that there really might be an end to winter after all. But I never would have seen the scuds if it weren't for the eyes of my fisherman husband. There was a miniscule and hidden world right in front of me, and I found it delightful to discover the lake in this new way.

So I bring you to Psalm 119:18:

> *Open my eyes that I may see wonderful things*
> *in your law.*

In Psalm 119, the longest chapter in the whole Bible, the psalmist is singing on and on about how great God's law is. But then he asks for his eyes to be opened. He doesn't feel like he has even begun to see the goodness in God's words.

I picture David and the Lord going to a thawing lake together. David sees how beautiful it is. He hears the birds, feels the breeze, smells the pines, and sees the water push against the reeds poking out of the lake. He's a musician, and he can write lyrics about his experiences all day long. But he's with the *creator* of the lake.

"Show me," he says. "Show me wonderful things here."

The Lord points and says, "Look at the scuds!"

David bends down. Sure enough. Tiny goodness in the water, and whole lessons about fish ecology and creatures he didn't even know existed.

Bible study is asking God to explain to you what *he* sees and being willing to bend down and look with him. It's a desire to be delighted by what delights him.

Before you even open your Bible, make this request: "Open my eyes!" Make it with enthusiasm and anticipation. Imagine yourself, not at a desk studying an ancient book, but rather at a lake with someone who has a unique perspective.

And hey, be encouraged that not even a Bible expert is going to be able to open this complex book and independently be able to see everything there is to see. We're all humbly reliant on the Author to open our eyes to the brilliant nuances in the text.

BIBLE STUDY TIP #3

Take lots of walk-throughs.

Matt and I used to live in a very old neighborhood. So old that the insulation in our home consisted of newspapers from the 1950s. During the summer, I loved to take walks in the cool mornings and look at the houses and the old trees that spread their canopies over the road. Eventually, I decided there were so many interesting house details to look at that I should be more intentional about seeing them.

So, one day I would take a walk and only look at front porches. The next day I would study the uniquely shaped and placed windows. The next day I looked at roof lines.

Then chimneys.

Then fish-scale shingles.

Then front doors.

Then walkways.

Then gardens and foliage.

And this, my friends, is the best way to study the Bible. Make several passes over the same Scripture passage, each time looking for unique information. It will give you a multi-faceted experience, and you will begin to see details you used to miss. Think of it like taking a walk through a beautiful old neighborhood.

Let's walk through Jeremiah 9:23-24. Grab paper and pencil and write "the LORD" at the top. It's good to decide what you're going to focus on and then make a list of facts you find in a passage, so as you read this time, list every detail you learn about the LORD.

This is what the LORD says: "Let not the wise boast of their wisdom or the strong boast of their strength or the rich boast of their riches, but let the one who boasts boast about this: that they have the understanding to know me, that I am the LORD, who exercises kindness, justice and righteousness on earth, for in these I delight," declares the LORD.

Remember, you're on a summer stroll. Relax now and enjoy the list you just made. Let the words roll around in your mind and sink into your heart.

P.S. We need a step counter for our strolls through the Bible. Somebody market that, would ya?

BIBLE STUDY TIP #4

Look up words in the original language.

Today you have to put up with the fact that I'm a high school Spanish teacher and love words. English is my first language, Spanish my second, and now I'm attempting Hebrew (although I'm starting to worry I'll never know more than the alphabet). One thing I've learned is that translations are great, but looking at the original language will often give you a depth of understanding that you just can't experience in the translation. Looking up words in the original language is like getting to the center of a hot cinnamon roll. It's worth your time.

Read Jeremiah 9:23-24 *again.* (Remember, we're slowly walking through one Scripture passage several times, looking for unique treasures with each pass.)

> *This is what the LORD says: "Let not the wise boast of their wisdom or the strong boast of their strength or the rich boast of their riches,*

but let the one who boasts boast about this:
that they have the understanding to know me,
that I am the LORD, who exercises kindness,
justice and righteousness on earth, for in these
I delight," declares the LORD.

See that word *LORD*? It's in all caps, because in the original Hebrew it has a special meaning that is different from *Lord* in lower case.

Come with me to my favorite Bible study website, and let me show you how easy it is to see the original language. Navigate online to https://www.blueletterbible.org/. Type in "Jeremiah 9:23-24," and then choose the translation you like.

See where the reference, Jeremiah 9:23, is in bold letters? Click on that. You'll see a popup window giving you the Hebrew spelling, audio of the Hebrew pronunciation, and English definitions for this word.

Scroll down and you'll see that *LORD* is actually *Jehovah*, which means "the existing one." Read even farther and see that it means "self-existent" and "eternal." We don't get that meaning from seeing "the LORD" in English.

Now you know that every time you see "the LORD" in all caps in the Old Testament, it means that he is the self-existent, eternal one.

If you have time, try looking up some of the other words in Jeremiah 9:23. Or try typing in one of your favorite verses in the Bible and see if you can gain any new insights by looking at the original language.

Hey Google, thanks for bringing Bible resources to us peasants.

BIBLE STUDY TIP #5

Look down for answers.

Today's tip is so simple that it seems ridiculous, yet it was something I had to be taught to do. I imagine you might need to learn this as well.

Very often, when someone has questions about God or the Bible, she looks up and taps her lips with her finger. (Would you mind actually doing this, so you get a feel for what I'm talking about?) That means she is looking for the answer *in her own mind*. For example, if she is wondering, "What is God like?" she'll think back to what she has already learned about God (whether it's true or not) or to her own opinion about God (whether it's true or not). Her response to the question will come from her own thinking.

When I was growing up, if I told my dad what I thought about something, he would say jokingly, "Be careful. With that apparatus you've got, it ain't safe." Maybe that's not such bad counsel. Very often what we think about things is incorrect.

As good students of the Bible, we want to be correct in what we learn, so we need to develop the habit of *looking down* at our Bibles and answering our questions based on biblical fact. Here's a practice question: "What is God like?"

Look down at Jeremiah 9:23-24 (I'll let you read this in your own Bible) and document three *biblically-based* facts about God, based on these verses.

1. God is:
2. God is:
3. God is:

Can you feel how much more solid your footing is, here on bedrock fact, rather than trying to come up with statements about God from your own thoughts?

P.S. Since I used to love it when the answers were at the back of my math book, here are the answers to the above questions:

1. God is LORD (eternal/self-existent).
2. God is kind.
3. God is just.

BIBLE STUDY TIP #6

Make a chart.

Have you ever looked at the same verse from five different angles? Well, it's happenin'!

Shout-out to all of you list lovers out there: Charts are helpful, because they allow you to turn a Bible verse into a more concrete list of facts. They also allow you to compare or contrastinformation. Of course, not every verse in the Bible lends itself to making a chart, but you can keep your eyes open for when it might work.

Grab your notebook and make a simple chart that looks like this:

DON'T BOAST ABOUT	DO BOAST ABOUT

Read Jeremiah 9:23-24, and fill in your chart with facts from these verses:

> *This is what the LORD says: "Let not the wise boast of their wisdom or the strong boast of their strength or the rich boast of their riches, but let the one who boasts boast about this: that they have the understanding to know me, that I am the LORD, who exercises kindness, justice and righteousness on earth, for in these I delight," declares the LORD.*

You're doing this Bible study work for relationship, so don't make a tidy chart and then rush off to your next task. Stay awhile. Pour a cup of hot coffee, and think about your chart while you're sipping.

BIBLE STUDY TIP #7

Apply truth to your life.

So far, you've done a good job gathering facts and also learning what "the LORD" means. Now it's time to ask, "So what do Jeremiah's words have to do with me?" It's really important to hold off on asking this question until you're sure you understand the verse. Often people read a verse and immediately try to apply it, which can mean they're acting on a weak or even false understanding. That would be like a detective walking into a crime scene and immediately declaring who the guilty party is before he has gathered physical evidence and interviewed witnesses. That shoddy work could lead to a false arrest. You want to be a good "detective" when you open the Bible.

So, after good fact-gathering, always ask these two questions:

1. What do I need to DO?
2. What do I need to BELIEVE?

Sometimes a verse will only answer one of these questions, but in the example below, you can answer both.

Read Jeremiah 9:23-24:

> *This is what the LORD says: "Let not the wise boast of their wisdom or the strong boast of their strength or the rich boast of their riches, but let the one who boasts boast about this: that they have the understanding to know me, that I am the LORD, who exercises kindness, justice and righteousness on earth, for in these I delight," declares the LORD.*

On paper, thoughtfully answer these questions:

1. What instruction do you receive from these verses? (If you want to be a wise person, what should you DO? What do you boast in now?)

2. What do you need to BELIEVE about the LORD? (Does any information in these verses contradict what you've thought about God before? If so, are you willing to change your beliefs to line up with the truth of the Bible?)

3. If you BELIEVE God is eternal, how does that affect your life? (How is it encouraging and hopeful?)

Just to remind you: the goal of Bible study isn't to make nice lists and charts so that you feel all smart. It's to help you get to a place where you can boast that you *know* God.

BIBLE STUDY TIP #8

Choose where to study.

A young woman recently asked me, "How do you even know where to study in the Bible? How do you choose a passage?" When you're looking at a compilation of sixty-six different books, even knowing where to open the Bible and begin can be intimidating.

Think about going to buy a new car. The salesman is going to want to know what you're looking for. Do you have six kids? You're going to be heading to the minivans. Do you have a long commute? You'll be looking at small, energy-efficient cars. Are you looking for thrills? Then you need a sports car with a convertible top and lots of horse-power.

So I'll ask you the same question. What are you looking for? Because there are different makes and models of books in the Bible. Let me give you a tour of some of your options:

Are you going through a rough patch? Head to the

Psalms, where David gives a raw look at his hard days but also reveals his solid relationship with God in the middle of it all.

Are you trying to figure out how to live your life? Go to Proverbs, where you get clear-cut pieces of wisdom: "Do this. Don't do that."

Are you trying to get to know Jesus? Read one of the testimonials about his life. These four books – Matthew, Mark, Luke and John – are called the Gospels. (*Gospel* means "good news.") I personally love the Gospel written by John, because it's super relational. In John, you'll see Jesus having a lot of conversations with people in different settings.

Do you need greater understanding of what it means to walk with Jesus? Head to any of the letters in the New Testament (the second half of the Bible – I'll explain more about that later.) You'll know they're letters because they mostly start out with "From Paul...to..." (except for Hebrews, which is a letter written by a mystery writer).

Do you want to know how this world got started and how God has been at work in the past? Go to the first five books in the Old Testament (the first half of the Bible.) Genesis, the very first book, is a great read.

Do you want to hear about God's interactions with the Israelites? Before Jesus came, there was a time when God spoke to his people through prophets. I love, love, love the book of Malachi. I'll take you there soon.

When you look at your literature options and choose where to study the Bible, keep in mind this truth from one of Paul's letters in the New Testament:

> *All Scripture is God-breathed and is useful...*
> *(2 Timothy 3:16)*

So relax. You cannot mess this up. If you decide to open the Bible, it's all going to be useful to you, no matter where you land. And remember that God wants you to know him. He wants your attention and devotion. He's honored when you want to spend time with him.

That said, if you still feel paralyzed by deciding what book to study in the Bible, I encourage you to make your default books Psalms and the Gospels. Not only are they straightforward and easy to understand, but you can live in those writings and never get to the bottom of the riches you'll find there.

Happy shopping.

BIBLE STUDY TIP #9

Refocus your attention.

A while back, someone asked me how I keep from getting distracted when I'm trying to study the Bible. Here's the only solution:

Stop being a human.

I consider myself to be a mature Christian with ingrained Bible study habits, but no one is more distractible than I am. The Lord is used to hearing me say, "Squirrel!" Just this morning, I had my quiet time supplies set out next to me on the couch and was meditating on a Scripture passage from Genesis. Next thing I knew, I was mentally rehearsing a Spanish lesson. What in the world?

You know what I do when that happens? I just say, "Come on, woman. Focus. FOCUS!" And I pick up where I left off in my Bible study. I have to do it every day.

EVERY DAY.

Here's the truth about God:

The LORD [see "the LORD" in all caps? You totally know what that means now!] is compassionate and gracious, slow to anger, abounding in love. (Psalm 103:8)

When I get distracted during my time with God, I know he has compassion on my humanity. He doesn't get mad easily, and if I'm willing to refocus my attention on him, he's for sure ready to give me grace, grace, grace. He's very kind.

So if you find yourself easily distracted, just relax. You are in a very big club. Refocus your attention and keep going. Don't do the guilt thing.

BIBLE STUDY TIP #10

Pay attention to pronouns.

When I was diagramming sentences in high school (which I thought was great fun), it never occurred to me that all of those details could help me understand the Bible. One of the ninja grammar skills we can use in Bible study is the ability to identify pronoun reference.

Pronouns are people, too!

Kidding. They don't always refer to people, but let's give them a little love and attention, eh?

If you're my age, it's been *decades* since you had to think about pronouns in an English class. Do you remember your pronouns? They are: I, you, he, she, it, we, they, y'all. (That last one is Texas flavored.)

Pronoun reference means that if I say "he," you know to whom I'm referring. If you read "they" in a Bible passage, do you know who "they" are? If you read "I" in a Bible passage, do you know who "I" is? If you get this wrong, you might end up misinterpreting the entire passage. It's a big deal!

For practice, read John 6:30:

> So they asked him, "What sign then will you give that we may see it and believe you? What will you do?"

Look at that verse, and identify to whom or what these pronouns refer:

1. THEY:
2. YOU:
3. IT:

Did you figure out all three? If you back up a few verses, to John 6:22-24, you see that *they* refers to a crowd of people who have been following Jesus around a lake. The pronoun *you* refers to Jesus. The pronoun *it* refers to the sign the crowd wants Jesus to give them.

Train yourself to slow up and think through pronoun reference *every time* you read the Bible. Good fact gathering leads to good understanding, which in turn leads to your life being transformed by the truth of Scripture.

BIBLE STUDY TIP #11

Get to know the people.

Recently I went to a Google Fest at the school where I teach, where I learned how to use the Google Keep app. I went in with my arms crossed because they promoted it as a replacement for sticky notes, and they were going to have to talk hard to convince me there is anything better in the whole world than a lovely, colorful stack of sticky notes to help me get things done.

Would you believe that I am now a Google Keep fanatic? Just watch me open my phone and view five or six to-do lists on one screen, all lined up in neat bullet points. If I check an item as done, it draws a line through that item and puts it down below in a light font. Love it!

The Bible, however, is not written in tidy, bulleted lists. Well, you have the ten commandments in Exodus and a few scattered other lists, and it's good to look for those places where you can chart things out. But usually the Bible is more like Instagram stories: candid moments in front of a video camera.

Real people.

Live.

Unedited.

In the Gospels, you have guys who sat around a campfire with Jesus. You wouldn't show up at a campfire with pencil and paper to take notes. Instead you would find a log to sit on, let the guys put a marshmallow on your stick, and absorb the conversation. You would take in all of the personalities and body language. You would consider the individual perspectives.

Often it's good to set aside your pencil and paper, and as you open the Bible, imagine that you're joining the group or at least eavesdropping on a conversation. Ask yourself this one question:

Who are these people?

Grab your Bible and read John 6:29-31. Last week we looked at pronoun reference, and we saw that "they" are a crowd of people who have been following Jesus around a lake. In verse 31, what is the back story of this crowd?

They had forefathers who ate manna in the dessert.

Okay, this isn't just any group of people. They're part of Israelite history. Last fall I got to walk through the land of Israel and eat my weight in hummus (not exaggerating.)

I walked around the same lake this crowd walked around. On one Sabbath, I sat in a congregation and worshiped with people who could say "our forefathers ate manna in the dessert with Moses." I was the outsider looking in.

This crowd of people following Jesus are Israelite. They had been waiting for generations to see the coming of their Messiah. Can you blame them for thinking he's going to provide an even more "wow" experience than their forefathers had with Moses in the wilderness?

If you have a good enough imagination, you might even be able to feel the crowd's hopeful, electric, desperate anticipation of the rescuer. You can hear them talking to each other. You can smell their sweat as they push in toward Jesus.

This is not a Bible passage designed for bullet lists on Google Keep.

Scripture is always about people and for people. If you think studying the Bible is challenging, it might be because you have to get used to finding out who God is through *story* instead of nice, tidy bullet points. Story always takes time and imagination and investment in getting to know the characters.

Be encouraged today. God cares more about people than lists.

BIBLE STUDY TIP #12

Don't confuse people's subjective perspective with God's objective perspective.

For ten years, while my kids were young, I did medical transcription from home. During that time, I picked up some mad keyboard speed and also learned a lot about the medical diagnostic progress. There's something in my experience that can help us in studying the Bible.

After a doctor would meet with a patient, he would go into his office, pick up a digital voice recorder, and describe everything that happened during his visit with the patient. That recording would end up on my desk to be transcribed.

There is a special format for doctor's reports called S.O.A.P. (Subjective, Objective, Assessment, Plan). The *subjective* section details what the patient says his symptoms are and what he thinks is wrong with his health. The *objective* section, which is the doctor's exam and fact gathering, is followed by the doctor's *assessment* of what is actually wrong with the patient, and the treatment *plan.*

I remember one time I took my husband into the emergency room because we were convinced he had appendicitis, but what he really had was a kidney stone. Our thoughtful subjective analysis of the situation did not match the more insightful objective analysis by the doctor.

When you're studying the Bible, keep in mind that this same scenario happens when people approach God. Especially listen to the conversations people have with Jesus, and you'll see their very limited *subjective* perspective on their situation versus Jesus' highly knowledgeable, fact-based, objective assessment of the situation.

For example, grab your Bible and read again the passage we've been looking at in John 6:25-35. In this passage, Jesus declares to the crowd that he knows they're only following him because he fed them bread earlier. (See John 6:1-15.) This reminds me of my college days when students would church-hop to whichever congregation was feeding college students that night.

Jesus tries to tell the crowd about a better kind of food, a better kind of bread, and they're all like, "Yeah, from now on give us this kind of bread!"

Jesus' response? "I aaaaaaaaaam the bread."

Now consider that Jesus is the best physician ever, and

listen to what his digital recording of this visit would sound like:

SUBJECTIVE: The crowd is hangry, as in stomachs growling and blood sugar dropping. They perceive physical hunger to be their problem.

OBJECTIVE: The crowd does appear to be malnourished.

ASSESSMENT: Diagnostics reveal chronic emptiness of soul. The crowd is a sea of empty hearts that need to be fed with something eternally nourishing.

PLAN: A complete change of diet recommended. Come to the Bread of Life, which is *not* found on the Wheat Montana Bakery shelf. Believe in Me and never experience soul hunger again.

As we read conversations between people and Jesus, we need to keep in mind that we are usually going to see two *very* different perspectives: what the person thinks he needs versus what Jesus, in his infinitely greater understanding, knows the person needs. As good Bible students, we can compare the subjective to the objective, and in doing so we'll probably see that our own subjective thinking needs to be adjusted to match Jesus' assessment of our situation.

One final thought: What kind of hungry are you?

BIBLE STUDY TIP #13

Bring the Bible into your language.

"Bad luck always comes in threes," I said.

Our senior pastor whipped his head around and replied, "We don't believe that. We don't believe in luck."

Wow. Chastisement received. I have never used that expression again.

Do you realize how many things we say in a day that have no biblical foundation whatsoever, or that even contradict what the Bible teaches? Part of Bible study should mean that what we read on the page becomes how we talk.

As a teacher, I am waging war against meaningless, damaging, unbiblical talk in my classroom. All summer long, I asked myself and the Lord if it was really worth it. Was I being ridiculous in asking my students to change their speech habits? Then I read an article for teachers that talked about the importance of all of the little things that happen within the classroom —actions and words that shape the environment of our room. So I put on my game face and have not let up in my daily gentle-but-firm preaching.

Let me give you an example: My students commonly say, "This sucks." But Paul has given believers this instruction:

> ...give thanks in all circumstances; for this is God's will for you in Christ Jesus.(1 Thessalonians 5:18)

The expression "This sucks" is not giving thanks. It's complaining.It's also a sharp, ugly expression, and Paul has told us to think about what's lovely and excellent. (See Philippians 4:8.) Thinking this way should result in lovely, good language.

"Please don't use that ugly expression in my class," I keep saying to my students. As a replacement, I offer them the expression "This is hard."

Bible study has to come with us into our day. It has to affect our thinking and the way we talk about *everything*. It should infuse us with hope so that we talk about hope. It should humble us so that we respond to people with humble words. It should shape our worldview, so that our conversation about world news is flavored with the truth of what God is doing on earth. It should convict us so that we apologize to people when we wrong them. It should fill us with gratitude so that we speak like grateful people. It should help us understand suffering so that we say joyful words when we go through trials.

God is a king, and he has high expectations for how people talk in his kingdom. The words we choose should never be controlled by how we *feel* in the moment, but should be completely controlled by what is *true* in the moment. And the words we use will be very strange compared to the words everyone else in the world is using.

I find that as I allow the Bible to dictate my speech, my speech dictates to my heart what my feelings should be. When I don't allow myself to say, "This sucks," but search for thankful words instead, in the process, my heart gets dragged along (sometimes kicking and screaming) towards gratitude. Even though it is seriously hard work, this is the transformation for which I long.

Every time you open your Bible, be ready to learn how to talk.

BIBLE STUDY TIP #14

Learn the meaning of "shalom."

When I was in Israel not too long ago, *shalom* was the common greeting – but it's more than just a friendly "hello." Because *shalom* is a Hebrew word used throughout the Old Testament, to understand this one word is to gain a deep knowledge about the heart of God and what he's trying to accomplish in our world.

Shalom means peace, which we usually think of as an absence of conflict. No enemies. No fighting. This can be part of it, but it also refers to an inner completeness, safety, tranquility, quiet, and contentment. One of the topics I write about often on my blog is worry, because I struggle with it so often. But I've been learning that God gives me what I need to leave worry behind and find a life of *shalom*. Who wouldn't gladly trade her inward state of churning anxiety for a state of wholeness and deep inner tranquility? Isn't everyone looking for that?

So I bring you to a profound verse in Judges 6. In this passage, the LORD has approached Gideon and is telling him to save Israel. (As if it's no big deal.) Gideon raises his eyebrows and says what we all would say, "Me? Are you kidding?" When he realizes he's talking to God himself, he really freaks out.

And then the LORD says to him, "Shalom."

> *So Gideon built an altar to the LORD there and called it The LORD is Peace. To this day it stands in Ophrah of the Abiezrites. (Judges 6:24)*

We hear Gideon saying that the LORD is peace (*shalom.*) God doesn't just give *shalom*, he IS *shalom*. This is what it means to know God: just being with him is to have *shalom* pour all over you all the time. And it's interesting to note that Gideon made his altar to the Lord before he did any of the risky, extreme actions God was telling him to do. He had an encounter with *shalom* before he saw everything turn out well.

What does this mean for us today? Experiencing *shalom* requires walking closely with God. We should practice worshiping the God who IS peace before we try to go out and live the life he wants us to live. We can build altars in our hearts and bow our knees to the one who can make us whole.

BIBLE STUDY TIP #15

Explore a small amount at a deep level.

In a culture where we want to measure things, it's easy to ask, "How much Bible study is enough?" If you study a whole chapter every day, is God going to be happy with you? Do you have to take a class with homework – is that what mature Christians do? How much? How much? How much?

I want you to toss out the idea of quantity and start thinking, *How deep?*

The further I go in my walk with Christ, I find myself wanting to study less and less of the Bible, in regard to quantity. Instead I want to let one rich verse sink in for days and transform the way I think and the way I live.

Let's go to Isaiah 26:3. Since it's good to stay put and go deep, we're going to spend a few chapters on one simple sentence.

You will keep in perfect peace those whose

minds are steadfast because they trust in you.

Such a short verse. Will you take a minute to memorize it?

Now, see the phrase "perfect peace"? That is *shalom*. We've learned that God IS *shalom*, and it's his own peace that drips all over us. But this *shalom* isn't for everyone. It's for the person whose mind is steadfast. I hope your curiosity is on fire: "Steadfast? What in the world does *steadfast* mean? Am I steadfast?"

(If you want a really rich Bible study life, get used to visiting blueletterbible.org and looking up the meaning of words in the original language. Remember to look up the verse and then click on the specific word to see a definition. Don't just Google the definition of the word, because it will give you the English definition instead of the Greek or Hebrew.)

Steadfast means "to rest upon or to lean against." I encourage you to grab a piece of paper and start making some notes about leaning against something. Here are the questions that come to my mind:

1. Why would a person lean on something?
2. If you need to lean against something, what does that say about you?
3. What does our American culture say about the

need to lean on something?

4. Is this a physical leaning against something, like you would lean against a wall or rest on a chair or against a desk? If not, then what does it mean?

5. What is the opposite of leaning?

6. Is my mind steadfast?

Okay, so you can see how we're sinking our brains and hearts down deep into this tiny little verse in Isaiah. And we're not done! We'll come to this verse again in the next three tips. Going through one verse four times: it's my favorite way to study the Bible.

BIBLE STUDY TIP #16

Ask WHERE.

You know what fun thing Matt and I are doing right now? We're trying to finish moving in with my mother-in-law, by cramming all of the belongings from our shed and garage into her garage. Ugh. She and her sister are in Arizona this month, so we have less than two weeks left to get things in order before they get back. I want them to smile when they drive in, but if you could see what the garage looks like right now, you would raise your eyebrows in skepticism that we can pull this off.

Stress.

But I am crazy hungry for the *shalom* available to me in relationship with God, so I keep putting Isaiah 26:3 to my mouth like an oxygen mask:

> *You will keep in perfect peace those whose minds are steadfast because they trust in you.*

In the last tip, we looked at the word *steadfast*, which means "to lean." Today's study tip is to ask, "Where?" Where do I lean? Does this verse answer that question? No, it doesn't. It tells us *why* we lean (which we'll look at in the next tip), but it doesn't tell us where.

But I still want an answer to that question, so I go elsewhere in the Bible, using the Bible itself as my resource for understanding Isaiah 26:3. If I go to blueletterbible.org and type in "lean," it brings up seven verses (in the NIV version of the Bible) with that word in it. Some of the verses talk about lean cows. Yeah, that's not really what I'm looking for. But Proverbs 3:5 is in the list of verses, and it answers the question, "Where?" (Doing this word search is a spiritual version of geocaching. We've just found treasure.)

Proverbs 3:5 says we shouldn't lean on our own understanding.

Where does leaning happen? On understanding. If I'm absolutely *not* to lean on my own understanding, then I must need an external understanding against which to lean. I think we can figure out from Isaiah 26:3 that it is God's understanding on which we're going to lean.

This makes me think. What's wrong with my own understanding that makes it so rickety? We could go exploring in the Bible to find great answers to that question, but for now, let's just assume that something is unreliable about my own understanding, so I need something sturdier on which to lean. Let me take this truth into my real life:

Last night I went to bed with tight shoulders and totally stressed about the garage chaos, but I reached out to *Shalom*. I rolled over, sank my head deep into the pillow and said, "Lord, to my understanding, this garage combining seems impossible, but in your way of thinking, nothing is impossible. I know you called us to live here, so I'm going to lean on your understanding of this moving situation." And with that I smiled like a person who has found a great secret to peace. *Shalom* was mine, and I drifted right to sleep.

So from exploring one tiny verse, we can find the big WHERE. Where does a person lean in order to experience peace? On an external understanding of life that is far superior to ours.

During the day, are you aware that you're leaning? Can you tell when you're leaning on your own understanding, and when you're leaning on God's? Next time you feel unsettled, anxious, or troubled, stand back and see which way you're leaning. This will explain your lack of inner *shalom*, and tell you how to find it.

Isn't it thrilling to stay in one spot in the Bible and dig deep?

BIBLE STUDY TIP #17

Ask WHY.

Wouldn't you say our time with Isaiah 26:3 has been like a piece of tiramisu? If you're a fan of *The Great British Baking Show*, then you can appreciate the labor that goes into creating perfect layers of rich sponge cake. To be a good student of the Bible, one has to slow down and savor the layers as well.

Today as we look at our final layer of Isaiah 26:3, my Bible study tip is to ask, "Why?"

> *You will keep in perfect peace those whose*
> *minds are steadfast because they trust in you.*

Why would someone remain steadfast by leaning his mind on the LORD? The answer from the text: Because he trusts in the LORD.

But WHY trust in the LORD?

Can you answer the above question just by *looking*

down at the information in this verse? (Say yes!) Think back a few chapters. What did we learn about the LORD? Remember that Gideon built an altar and named it "The LORD is Peace." He IS *Shalom*.

Why lean on the Lord's understanding of everything? Because his very essence is peace itself. Where else could we possibly lean and find a source of peace? Certainly not on our own understanding! And I don't know anyone else who actually IS completely *Shalom*. If peace is what we're after, there's simply no better place to lean our minds than on the Lord.

Now let's review the layers of truth we've savored in Isaiah 26:3:

1. "Perfect peace" is *shalom*, an inner wholeness.
2. The LORD IS peace.
3. The LORD can keep a person in peace.
4. "Steadfast" means to lean.
5. We can lean our minds on our own understanding or on the LORD's understanding.
6. The person who leans his thinking on God's understanding will be kept in *shalom*.
7. The reason a person would lean on God's understanding is that God IS *shalom*.

Do you see the full circle of reasoning in this verse?

Grab a piece of paper, write out Isaiah 26:3, and these seven truths underneath the verse. The next time you feel anything but peaceful, you can mentally walk through these truths. This exercise will give your mind a big push to lean the right way. You'll be moving toward *Shalom*.

Peace out.

BIBLE STUDY TIP #18

Keep in mind God's attitude towards us.

In the early years of my marriage, there was a moment every day when I was convinced Matt didn't care about me – maybe didn't even love me. It was in the morning when I bent down to pick up his dirty socks off of the floor (again!) and put them in the hamper.

Then one day, I realized that actually he was just taking off his socks at night because it felt good. He was dropping them on the floor because the floor was nearby. End of story. There was no evil intent on his part. In fact, he was very caring and loving toward me all day, every day.

This same kind of scenario can happen when we read the Bible. We might look at a passage that is difficult to understand or weird or seemingly harsh. We draw a conclusion: God must not care – maybe he doesn't even love us.

But that's not true.

No matter how a certain verse or story might seem, I

urge you to keep in mind the truth about God's attitude towards us. Take a minute to look up these passages containing a few staple truths on which you can lean your mind:

1. God is mindful of men. (Psalm 8:3-4)
2. God has a kindly intent toward and even delights in people. (Luke 2:14) You won't get the full meaning just by looking at the English, so go to blueletterbible.org and study the words in this verse.
3. God continually demonstrates his love for us by something incredible he did on our behalf. (Romans 5:8)
4. God is for us. (Romans 8:31)

I want to take this a step further and say that no matter what is happening in *your* story right now, focus on the truth of God's attitude towards you. Even if life is hard, God is daily showing his love for you by what Jesus did for you on the cross. He is mindful of you. (You're never forgotten!) He has nothing but goodwill toward you and even delights in you. He is in your corner.

Try reading through the above list of facts every time you open your Bible this week, *before* you read anything else. Feel God's warmth toward you as you approach him.

I think you'll find it takes the word "study" out of Bible study and turns your reading into an encouraging, loving encounter instead.

If you come upon a hard passage, default back to remembering how God feels about people: We are loved.

BIBLE STUDY TIP #19

Let Bible stories inform your perspective on life.

Last night I went to a choir concert for the Christian school where I teach. Despite the stifling heat in the gym, I enjoyed the music. The middle school choir sang "Battle of Jericho," which I've heard more times than I can count. But this time, my mind went back to our Israel trip and I thought, *Oh my word, the battle of Jericho – real place, real event.*

Recently, I have been concerned for Israel, as Hamas violently rages against Israel's southern border. My prayers have kept surfacing, for the Lord to watch over the Israeli Defense Force. Now that I know the faces and even the names of soldiers, their safety is on my mind.

Joshua "fit the battle of Jericho" all of those years ago, on God's orders. The people of Israel marched, and the walls came "tumbling down." But I now know that Israel doesn't do wrought iron or timber walls. She is a land of stones – huge, chiseled stones from quarries. Stones that don't just tumble down without the exertion of some immense force.

I sat at that concert, listened to the music, and connected the battle of Jericho to the current situation in Israel. I thought, *If God can bring down the stone walls of a city in Israel, he can protect its borders and its soldiers now.*

In Malachi 3:6, we read God's declaration about himself: *I the LORD do not change.*

God does not change, which means that whatever he was able to pull off at the time of Joshua, he is able to pull off now. Whatever he cared about then, he cares about now. So read the amazing, should-be-a-movie stories of the Bible and extract truth that you can apply to your situation now. Let Bible stories inform your perspective on life.

In my case, I know God wanted his people to take back the land of Israel in the time of Joshua, and he still wants them to own this land today. Recently Israel celebrated seventy years of independence. What a miracle of God that they became a nation once again! Surely he can protect Israel from her enemies today.

Sometimes I think believers feel like they need to outgrow the exciting Bible stories they heard as a little kid and go on to "deeper" lessons, but I say "Nuh-uh." The exciting Bible stories are where it's at, and they're gloriously simple to read and understand. Maybe you'll struggle to understand the deep theological lessons written by Paul, but everybody can understand that because of God, Moses and the Israelites escaped Egypt and crossed the sea on dry land, because of God, David killed Goliath, and because of God, Jesus stood outside of a tomb, said, "Come out!" and the dead guy walked out.

How about this: If you get frustrated reading a hard-to-understand text in the Bible, take a break and go borrow your preschooler's illustrated *Jesus Storybook Bible*. Read an epic story, feel the wow factor, tell God he's *so cool*, and call it a legit Bible study.

Have faith like a kid. Because that's what Jesus said we should do, we never walk too far away from the stories that make our eyes grow wide. This is Bible study. Enjoy the awesome.

BIBLE STUDY TIP #20

Let the Bible define you.

In my childhood home, we had a wall of black bookcases in the living room, and at the end of one was a dictionary. It was a normal event, when my parents came upon a word they didn't know or a definition of a word they couldn't agree on, that one of them would get up and grab the dictionary. Then we would have school for a few minutes.

Bible study is all about words. I've had you looking up word definitions on the newfangled internet instead of in a hard-copy dictionary, but sometimes you need to open your Bible like it's the dictionary and look for a definition of YOU.

1. Who are you?
2. What does your life mean?
3. What is your value?

For months, I have been building a stack of note cards, with a top card entitled "The Truth about Me." Just a few days ago, I came to some verses that I had to add to my collection:

> *Since, then, you have been raised with Christ, set your hearts on things above, where Christ is, seated at the right hand of God. Set your minds on things above, not on earthly things. For you died, and your life is now hidden with Christ in God. When Christ, who is your life, appears, then you also will appear with him in glory. (Colossians 3:1-4)*

Go back and read that again, looking at all the pronouns directed to followers of Christ, which is *you*. (I told you that pronouns matter!)

1. You have been raised with Christ.
2. You died.
3. Your life is now hidden with Christ in God.
4. Christ is your life.
5. You will appear with him in glory.

I highly recommend memorizing these verses, so your brain can marinate in these incredible ideas. If you're trying to find out who you are in this life, the Bible is an external, reliable source of information. It drips hope all over your personal identity.

BIBLE STUDY TIP #21

*Use the Bible to clarify your past,
define your present, and inform your future.*

Today was a warm day, and I was desperate to keep my Spanish students awake for a while, so they lined up in teams and did speed relays in verb conjugation. If you're going to be a good Bible student, you have to care about verbs because verb tense tells us *when* an action takes place.

Let's revisit the passage we looked at last, this time looking only at verb tense:

> *Since, then, you have been raised with Christ, set your hearts on things above, where Christ is, seated at the right hand of God. Set your minds on things above, not on earthly things. For you died, and your life is now hidden with Christ in God. When Christ, who is your life, appears, then you also will appear with him in glory. (Colossians 3:1-4)*

This passage lends itself to making lists, so, while focusing on verbs, let's divide the information based on *when* the actions occurred.

PAST:You have been raised with Christ.

You died.

PRESENT: Your life is now hidden with Christ in God.

Christ is your life.

FUTURE:You will appear with Christ in glory.

Let me ask you a question: Was there a time in your past when you died to yourself and were raised to life with Christ? Do you even know what that means?

If you do have new life in Christ, how aware are you of this whole "hiddenness" thing? This was a brand new idea to me when I discovered it recently in Sara Hagerty's book, *Unseen: The Gift of Being Hidden in a World That Loves to be Noticed.* Since then, I've tried to imagine myself being tucked away in this hidden, safe place in Christ.

Did you ever watch the movie *Hidalgo?* The main character barely outruns a sandstorm on his horse, taking shelter in some ruins just as the blast of sand hits the walls. It's intense. That's what I picture when I think of being hidden in Christ.

As for the future, can you imagine a place called "glory" where you will appear with Christ? Sounds really nice to me about now, because not all is glorious in my life.

Most people don't make much effort to know the biblical truth about who they were, are, and will be. But you're memorizing these verses, yes? Chewing on them? Letting the truth drip into all the empty places in your poor ego?

Maybe you need to do what I've done and invest in some 3x5 cards, so you can start a collection of Bible truths about yourself. My stack is thick and quickly becoming dog-eared, because I've read through it so many times.

You need help, when your self-perception is all wonky, to know who you were, are, and will be.

BIBLE STUDY TIP #22

Look for commands.

A few days ago, I sat by myself in the waiting room of the hospital imaging center. Matt was undergoing an MRI for some neck pain, and I had forty minutes of quiet and solitude to let my thoughts run wild about what the MRI would reveal.

As I sat there, Colossians 1:3-4 came to mind:

> *Since, then, you have been raised with Christ, set your hearts on things above, where Christ is, seated at the right hand of God. Set your minds on things above, not on earthly things. For you died, and your life is now hidden with Christ in God. When Christ, who is your life, appears, then you also will appear with him in glory. (Colossians 3:1-4)*

Because I had labored for a few weeks to memorize

this passage, I was able mentally to continue my study of Paul's words while I waited. I marveled at the fact that, even though my body was in the imaging center, my life was actually at the right hand of the throne of God, tucked away in Christ. Then I turned my attention to the three commands Paul gives in these verses, commands that make sense in light of where my life is now:

1. Set your hearts on things above.
2. Set your minds on things above.
3. Don't set your minds on earthly things.

These commands sat like companions with me in the waiting room. Friends. One looked at me and said, "Your husband's life is in Christ. Your life is in Christ. Bodies will waste away, but your lives are eternal. Rest your heart in this."

The other leaned over and said, "I can tell your mind is going to worrisome places, imagining worst-case scenarios for your husband, but lift your thoughts to the throne. Your life is hidden in the Healer. You're right next to the Creator, the one who breathes life. No matter what, everything is going to be okay."

The third said sternly, "Stop thinking that this earth and these bodies are all there is."

The waiting room turned into a chapel, and my heart

and mind calmed. This is Bible study. So look for the commands in the Bible and collect them like precious friends, who will come with you into every situation and speak good words in your ear. Do what they say and experience the good life.

BIBLE STUDY TIP #23

Examine the book jacket.

I told you a while ago that I would take you to one of my favorite places in the Bible – the book of Malachi. This is as generous as a Montana native being willing to disclose the location of his favorite huckleberry patch.

Of the sixty-six books of the Bible, there are quite a few that come right out, in the beginning, and let you know what the book is about, who's writing the book, and to whom the author is writing. Malachi is one of these. That leads me to today's Bible study tip: Examine the book jacket.

If you pick up a new book, you flip it over to read the author bio, the endorsements, and the blurb. Before you've even read the first chapter of the book, you already have some idea of what you're heading into. You can do this with books of the Bible, when the first few sentences give you a lot of contextual clues. For example, read the "book jacket" of Malachi:

> *The oracle of the word of the LORD to Israel*
> *through Malachi. (Malachi 1:1 NASB)*

We can make a list of facts from this introductory verse.

FACT #1: THIS BOOK IS AN ORACLE.

Stop! Please tell me your curiosity won't let you go any further until you know what "oracle" means. Go to blueletterbible.org (Can you tell that I live at this website?) and look up Malachi 1:1. Click on "Malachi 1:1" and then scroll down and click on the number "H4853" next to the word *oracle*. You'll see that the word literally means "burden." Read on down, and you'll see that figuratively it means an "uttered doom." So as you head into Malachi, brace yourself. This isn't going to be a fun, light read. However, though it's a weighty, hard message, it's also very rich and enlightening.

FACT #2: THIS BOOK IS A WORD OF THE LORD.

Just a reminder: "LORD" in all caps is "Jehovah" in Hebrew – the proper name for the one true God. It means "self-existent" or "eternal." It seems fitting that we would hear God's proper, imposing name as he's getting ready to speak a heavy word.

Fact #3: God's relationship with Israel is important to your own faith in Christ.

As you read Malachi, you'll get to know God, but only as you see him in relationship with Israel. In Romans 1:16, Paul says, *"For I am not ashamed of the gospel, because it is the power of God that brings salvation to everyone who believes: first to the Jew, then to the Gentile."* As Gentiles reading Malachi, we must approach the book with humility. It is only by God's kindness and generosity that Israel's Scriptures are now part of our own spiritual heritage.

Fact #4: The word of the LORD is coming to Israel through Malachi.

This first verse is the only time Malachi is mentioned in the book that bears his name. He is simply God's mouthpiece to deliver a weighty message. Try going to good old Wikipedia and reading about Malachi. You can get a quick idea of what his name means and the time frame in which he wrote.

Does this book jacket pique your interest? Don't you want to know what the LORD has to say to his chosen people? It's astounding, really, that the Eternal God cares to speak to men, especially to this little speck of a nation, Israel. A lot of world philosophies would tell us that God is far off and unapproachable or that the creator of this planet set it spinning and then walked away. But this is not true.

The LORD comes in close and speaks to people. He is relational, and this is encouraging. Even if the message is going to be burdensome, at least it's from a God who cares enough to see and to communicate with his own people.

I'm going to bring you back to Malachi for several chapters, so I encourage you to stop and pray right now. Don't read any further in the book. Instead, ask God what he wants to show you through this prophecy by Malachi. The same LORD who spoke to Israel wants to speak to you through his word.

BIBLE STUDY TIP #24

Learn the historical context.

I so badly want to grab your hand and ask you to jump into the book of Malachi, but we need to make one stop before we do that. Let's look at the historical context of the book. (Did you yawn when I said "historical"?) We owe it to the Israelites to get a handle on what life has been like for them, before reading the heavy word that God is sending their direction.

Start with a Google search of "historical context of Malachi." I particularly liked the article by ESV.org. Do you know what sticks out to me in this article? The Israelites feel disappointed. They got their hopes up and so far *nothing*. In their season of waiting and growing disappointment, we're going to see what has happened in their lives. Look at this one promise they had been hanging onto:

> *"Shout and be glad, Daughter Zion. For I am coming, and I will live among you," declares*

the Lord. (Zechariah 2:10)

They're all ready to shout and more than ready to be glad, but where is the LORD?

You know this feeling, right? Waiting. Hoping. Disappointment. *Nothing.* What happens in your heart and mind during a season like this? What happens to your relationship with God? What happens to your worship and your service and your giving and your relationships?

It's always tempting, when we read the Old Testament especially, to approach it from a great distance and make judgments on the people and their flaws, but the inner struggle of the Israelites is a human struggle that still plagues us today. We all easily lose hope when God delays in keeping his promises. So as you read Malachi, put yourself in the shoes of the Israelites, who just want life to be good right now. Maybe their story isn't so different from yours.

BIBLE STUDY TIP #25

Consider the literary style.

I'm going to ask you to do something that's going to sound very English-teachery. We're going to look at literary style. As we do, keep in mind that I took Shakespeare in high school *for fun*. As Macbeth would say, "Screw your courage to the sticking place," and we will talk about literature for a few minutes.

The book of Malachi is one of my favorites because of the style in which it's written. Will you puleeease take a few minutes to read the whole book? When I say "book," I don't mean the 1,225 pages of *War and Peace*, I mean the four chapters of Malachi that only fill two pages in the Bible. As you read, consider how unique the style of this book is. No other book of the Bible is written in the same way.

How would you describe the literary style of this book? To me it has a parent-to-naughty-teenager feel or maybe you would describe it as a courtroom style of writing, with indictments, prosecution, and defense.

This is a great place to make a list. Check out all of the questions coming from the children of God:

1. How have you loved us? (1:2)
2. How have we shown contempt for your name? (1:6)
3. How have we defiled you? (1:7)
4. Why [don't you pay attention to our offerings]? (2:13-14)
5. How have we wearied [the LORD]? (2:17)
6. How are we to return [to you]? (3:7)
7. How are we robbing you? (3:8)
8. What have we said against you? (3:13)

This feels like teaching high school. "Stop doing that," I say.

"What? What was I doing?" says the teenager, with innocent eyes, but guilt dripping from every pore of his body. Busted. (That would be a great alternate title for the book of Malachi.)

I say, "You know what." Accompanied by my best mean-teacher look.

This book is a long list of heavy accusations from the Lord, but I'm still impressed that he's willing to have the conversation. Hatred turns its back on a person, maybe even walks away in frustration, but love keeps us face to face. Love confronts and explains and dives into the hard talk. Love fields the questions and lets the other person be honest.

By considering the literary style, we have found a starting place from which to approach this interesting book. Read through the above list of questions a few more times. Get a feel for where the children of Israel are in their relationship to God. Malachi is a really old book, but maybe in places it feels more relevant than we care to admit. Feeling the rhythm of literary style of rhetorical questions in this book can help you get a feel for the heart of God and the heart of the people.

BIBLE STUDY TIP #26

Face the hard passages.

Imagine that a bowl of trail mix is in front of you. What kind of person are you? Do you grab a handful and eat it all, or are you one of those miscreants who stands by the bowl and only picks out the M&Ms? Confess! And please know that if I catch you picking the chocolate out of the mix, I am going to holler at you and probably whack your hand. Consider yourself warned.

Now think of Bible study as trail mix.

There are the salty, interesting passages and the sweet, easy-to-digest passages of the Bible, and then there are the raisins – those passages that are just weird or disturbing or seemingly impossible to understand. Nobody likes raisins.

But we need the *whole Bible*, not just the easy, pleasant parts. So here's today's Bible study tip:

Don't be an M&M picker.

Or, in other words: Face the hard passages.

The oracle from Malachi starts off with a big raisin. The LORD says he has loved Israel, but Israel asks, "How?" How has God loved us? We don't want to miss this, because isn't this a core question that we all need answered? Before we read the answer, let's remember that Malachi hasn't crafted his words for the Hallmark greeting card department. This is an oracle – a heavy message. We should expect a weighty, probably unpleasant conversation here.

> *"Was not Esau Jacob's brother?" declares the Lord. "Yet I have loved Jacob, but Esau I have hated, and I have turned his hill country into a wasteland and left his inheritance to the desert jackals." (Malachi 1:2b-3)*

Hmmm.

Do you know what's hard about this? Jacob and Esau aren't part of our history as Gentiles. The LORD is talking to Israel, and the story of Jacob and Esau is *Israel's* history. The Israelites are familiar with these men the way an American is familiar with George Washington and Paul Revere. While the names of Jacob and Esau immediately mean a lot to the Israelite audience, without any explanation, we have to make more effort to understand.

Take time to read Genesis 25:19-34 and chapter 27. Let Jacob and Esau's story sink in.

Now let me tell you what I do with a hard passage like this one in Malachi. There are tools for understanding it more deeply, but before exploring those options, I roll around the verses in my mind and pray about what they mean. Here I could ask, "Father, why are you explaining your love by way of Jacob and Esau? What is it about your relationship with these two brothers that expresses something profound to Israel?" I keep asking and asking and asking that question. I let curiosity burn and fuel my desire to understand the message God is trying to get across to his people.

It's okay *not* to understand Scripture right away. Be patient and just sit with the hard verses for a long time. Read them over and over again. Try not to make guesses about the meaning, and don't jump to conclusions. Take time to put yourself in Israelite shoes, considering their history and their current circumstances. Why are they even wondering if God really loves them?

We'll come back to this passage next week, after you've had time to sit with it.

Let me finish with a quote from my husband: "Hard isn't bad; it's just hard."

Eat the raisins.

BIBLE STUDY TIP #27

Follow the cross-references.

Hey, I've promised you fifty-two Bible study tips, and we're halfway there. If you lived nearby, I would buy an assortment of donuts and have you over to celebrate. (I get the maple bar.)

On my seventeenth birthday in 1986, my parents presented me with a burgundy leather-bound Bible. On the inside, in my mother's perfect cursive, is written, "This Bible was presented to Christy Denise Willenbrecht on the 26th day of January, 1986." (That was back when my last name was 12 letters long.) I still have this Bible, except now the leather has a hard-earned patina, and the binding is showing at one end of the spine. It weighs a good three pounds, and it's filled with study helps that I had no idea how to use when I was seventeen years old.

One of my favorite study tools is smooshed into the center column of each page, looking like one of those complicated things that anyone with common sense would ignore. I'm talking about the cross-references. When you're reading along in the text, sometimes you see a tiny letter in superscript next to a word. (At my age now, I need readers to see these.) If you follow that verse number and the letter in superscript into what I'm going to call the "cream-filled center" of the study Bible page, you'll see a few other verses listed there. These verses are related in some way to the word you've just seen in the verse you were reading. Follow these supplemental verses and you'll see how the Bible interconnects. You'll discover how one verse gives meaning to another. Using the cross-references is a way for you to use the Bible itself to help you study the Bible.

Let's go to Malachi 1:2-3. In my three-pound study Bible, I discovered the tiny letters "a" and "b" within the text. Next I went to the center-column cross-references and looked for verses 2-3.

For a refresher, here's Malachi 1:2-3:

> *"I have loved you," says the Lord.*
> *"But you ask, 'How have you loved us?'"*
> *"Was not Esau Jacob's brother?" declares the*
> *Lord. "Yet I have loved Jacob, but Esau I have*
> *hated, and I have turned his hill country into*

a wasteland and left his inheritance to the desert jackals."

For Malachi 1:2a, I found these supplemental verses:

Deuteronomy 4:37

Deuteronomy 7:8

Deuteronomy 23:5

Isaiah 41:8-9

Jeremiah 31:3

John 15:12

For Malachi 1:2b, I found this supplemental verse:

Romans 9:13

For Malachi 1:3, I found these supplemental verses:

Jeremiah 49:10, 16-18

Ezekiel 35:3, 4, 7, 8, 15

Now what you need is coffee, your favorite doughnut from my celebration box, and half an hour. Time to go exploring, to see if any of these verses give you clues about *how* the LORD has loved Israel. Grab your notebook, to list the facts as you read.

Reading these passages might leave you with more questions than answers, but you are on a journey here. Because there's no way to tackle this hard passage in Malachi without going through a process of detailed study, you have to decide if you care enough to put in the work or if you only want to read the easy passages for the rest of your life. And as you go through this process, will you take a minute to appreciate the preacher at your church? I know my husband, Matt, spends hours wrestling with hard passages before he dares present them as a message for our congregation.

Next time, I'm going to zoom in on one of those supplemental passages and compare it to Malachi 1:2-3, but for now you're on your own. Why don't you go ahead and enjoy feeling smart, as you get comfortable using cross-references?

BIBLE STUDY TIP #28

Let God be who he says he is.

Matt was offering me his last waffle fry at Chick-Fil-A, when I said to him, "Well, it's time for me to get home and write Bible study tip #28. Gotta take my own advice and keep looking at this hard passage in Malachi." I've been asking him if he thinks I'm very brave to tackle this, and he says I am.

Today we continue to let Israel's question to God haunt us: "How have you loved us????"

God answers with a weird explanation that Esau was Jacob's brother, but he loved Jacob and hated Esau. This answer leaves me with my eyes squinched and mouth slack. I have muscle memory of this facial expression from every math class I ever took. It's my "This makes no sense and why am I even here?" face.

But let's just take a recess from all that is hard and remember Bible study tip #18: Keep in mind God's attitude towards us. I'm about to take you to a verse that we looked up as a cross-reference last time, and I warn you that it might feel cold and uncomfortable. But let's breathe deeply from John 3:16, which tells us that God loves the world. He loves the *whole* world and sent his Son to die for the salvation of anyone willing to believe. If you start to freak out, let this be your fall-back verse.

Okay, with the cross-references we went to Romans 9:13, where we see Paul quoting Malachi (probably from memory, being a good Pharisee): *"I have loved Jacob, but Esau I have hated."*

We talked about how hard this passage is for us Gentiles to understand. I mean, Jacob and Esau aren't from our own history. It's super helpful that Paul, who is Jewish and hyper-trained in the Hebrew Scriptures, quotes this verse like it's no big thing. So we can ask, "Okay, Paul. What in the world?"

First, we have to zoom out to see what he is talking about. Take a few minutes to read all of Romans 9, and then imagine describing it to a friend in your own words.

Look at Romans 9:2: *"I have great sorrow and unceasing anguish in my heart."* In this chapter, Paul is moaning over the welfare of his own people. Then read the list of what he says the Jews have: adoption as sons, the divine glory, covenants, law, temple worship, promises, patriarchs, and the very line of ancestry to Messiah.

But they have rejected the Messiah.

Paul is doubled over in pain. His people have had everything from God, yet they have refused the Messiah God has sent. Now the Gentiles are readily accepting the Jewish Messiah, while most of the Jews blindly keep trying to be righteous by works instead of faith in the Messiah.

In the middle of Paul's wailing is the whole Jacob/Esau thing. Hmmm. (When you're wrestling with a hard passage, you should say "Hmmm" a lot. Let's call that Bible study tip #28b.)

Let's skip over verses 13 and 14, and read Romans 9:15, where God tells Moses that he'll have mercy on whomever he wants. This is where Bible study tip #28 comes in: Let God be who he says he is. Let me say these words to you again: *"God will have mercy on whom he wants."* Look at the crazy example Paul gives, and you tell me if this doesn't feel all kinds of uncomfortable: Way back in the day, God used Pharaoh for his own purpose, and he hardened Pharaoh's heart toward Israel. Then we read in Romans 9:18 that God has mercy on whomever he wants and hardens whomever he wants.

Ugh. Does anybody want to think about this aspect of God?

God has mercy on whomever he wants and hardens

whomever he wants. Right now in your Bible study you have to decide, "Am I going to believe this truth about God, even though I may not like it?"

All right, guys – are y'all still with me? (Sometimes when I'm thinking really hard about a difficult passage, it feels like my brain is going to explode.) Back to this Jacob/Esau thing: before these twins were born, God decided that Esau would serve Jacob. How does this show Israel God's love?

Because God chose Jacob.

God chose to be merciful toward Jacob and his descendants. That's the love. The only reason Israel belongs to God is because God decided to show mercy to this nation. Why didn't God choose it to be the other way around? Why not Esau and his line as the chosen nation and Jacob and his people serving Esau? *Only because of God's choice.*

My opinion? Israel should be releasing a big *phew* upon hearing these words. *Phew, we're glad it was us. We don't know why God chose to be merciful toward us, but we'll take the love.*

Let's recap the actions we took in tackling this hard-to-understand verse in Malachi:

1. We used cross-references to find related Scripture verses.

2. We spent time zooming in on one particular reference that seemed to give helpful information.

3. We read the whole chapter surrounding that reference and got a feel for the context.

4. Then we went back to our original question and tried to answer it: How did God show love to Israel by loving Jacob and hating Esau?

5. We decided whether we were going to believe the new aspect of God's character that we discovered in doing this research.

Are you still left with questions about all of this? That's okay! Just keep thinking and praying. Sometimes it takes a while before God really helps us understand the depth of what he has to say. No worries. Today was a great start. Well begun is half done!

Now come on over and get a Fudgsicle, you guys, because I think we have worked up a sweat today.

BIBLE STUDY TIP #29

Keep the hard passage open in your tabs.

This could be a fun survey, for you all to tell me how many tabs you have open on your computer most of the time. I have three open right now, but that's a low number for me. (My brother wins with half a kajillion open. It makes me break into hives just to look at all of them.) We keep tabs open, because we want to get back quickly to something we were looking at, and I think that is a great Bible study tip: Keep the hard passage open in your tabs.

Last time, we looked at the "How have you loved us?" question in Malachi 1:2, and maybe you're still struggling with the answer: God has mercy on whomever he wants to have mercy, and it so happens that he chose to be merciful toward Jacob and his descendents. Could you keep that tab open while we go to a new one in Malachi? Let's swing to the second half of Malachi 1:14:

"...For I am a great king," says the LORD Al-

mighty, "and my name is to be feared among the nations."

A great king.

It wasn't until I devoured *The Lord of the Rings* trilogy by J.R.R. Tolkien that I began to absorb what *king* meant. A friend said I should watch those movies for the richness of themes and relationships, but I thought the whole hobbits and elves thing was just weird. Finally he talked me into it, but I insisted on reading all three books before watching the movies. You guys, I read all three books and watched all three movies in ONE MONTH, at which point I temporarily lost connection with reality and felt like Middle Earth was a real place and I was seeing Frodo "with my waking eyes."

Because the trilogy is set in the times of kings, I started feeling how very different kingdoms are from democracies. Kings do whatever they want, and there's no voting them out in four years. Kings aren't public servants. Kings speak and subjects obey. Kings are revered and bowed down to. Kings show mercy to whomever they want to show mercy.

God says he is not only a king but a great king. Maybe this is why I love Malachi so much. What does it mean to serve a king? This seems both terrifying and wonderfully majestic to me. In *Renovation of the Heart*, Dallas Willard says, "The kingdom of God is the range of God's effective will, where what God wants done is done."[1]

Now toggle screens. Look at the fact that God is a great king, and then toggle back to the hard passage and the statement that he has loved Israel by loving Jacob and hating Esau. More mercy toward one brother? Seems unfair until we say out loud, "God is a great king, and in his kingdom what he wants done is done."

Can an entitled American living in a democracy even begin to understand kingdom rule? Can we bend our knees to a king and accept his will without receiving "I voted" stickers for our shirts? Can we sing that God is our king and really mean it?

I went to blueletterbible.org and typed in "king" – and found gold. There was a song that Israel should have been singing, but maybe in the days of Malachi they had stopped singing it altogether:

> *For the Lord Most High is awesome,*
> *the great King over all the earth.*
> *He subdued nations under us,*
> *peoples under our feet.*
> *He chose our inheritance for us,*
> *the pride of Jacob, whom he loved.(Psalm 47:2-4)*

Here's a challenge for you today: Look at the hardest circumstance in your life and then contemplate the fact that God is a great king. What does that mean for you in this situation? Will you sing the praises of this king?

BIBLE STUDY TIP #30

Become a collector.

Matt was recently mocking my large collection of salt and pepper shakers, but I ignored him completely. Actually, I have two more collections as well. At Christmas time I set out a fun Santa collection – my favorite being the Santa made out of a small stick of driftwood. Then in January, I display a collection of snowmen, and those stay up until March 1st, when I optimistically take them down in hopes of a spring that won't really come to Montana until May.

Collecting means you enjoy and value something, so you keep your eyes open for items that fit the theme but are unique and add their own character to the collection. This is today's Bible study tip: Become a collector.

Let's use Malachi 1:14b as the seed for a collection:

> "...For I am a great king," says the LORD Almighty, "and my name is to be feared among the nations."

If God is a king, we should start accumulating knowledge about his kingdom. At this point, you're going to need an oversized Rubbermaid to store your collection. Make sure it has a handle and wheels.

If you go to blueletterbible.org (is this website feeling like home yet?) and type in "kingdom," a boatload of references come up. In reading through them, it doesn't take long to see that there are kingdoms of men and then there's the kingdom of God. Read the following sampling of verses and take notes about the kingdom of God:

> Psalm 45:6
>
> Psalm 103:19
>
> Isaiah 9:7
>
> Daniel 4:2-3
>
> Matthew 4:23
>
> Acts 14:22
>
> Colossians 1:12-13
>
> Hebrews 12:28
>
> Revelation 12:10

In an article posted by oneforisrael.org, I learned that "it's a very Jewish approach to Bible study" to take a word and "look sideways...scanning the Scriptures for other instances that give meaning to that concept in the light of how it appears elsewhere." [2]

Collecting means appreciating the beautiful and unique artistry that can surround one theme. Collectors are always looking for new additions, and this search is rooted in pure enjoyment. Of course, the upside to being a collector in Bible study is that you never have to dust anything.

Now, don't you want to go add to your "kingdom" collection?

BIBLE STUDY TIP #31

Tally the repeats.

This Wyoming girl had a hoity-toity moment in Amsterdam about a decade ago. While I was with a team of people going to Uganda, we had a long layover in Amsterdam. We left the airport for a few hours and rode a train through the city, passing classic Dutch waterways, so many people riding bicycles, and the home where Anne Frank hid with her family during World War II.

Then we arrived at the National Museum, where I was enthralled to walk right up to Rembrandt paintings hanging on the walls. *Rembrandt!* They weren't even roped off or anything – just hanging there like they would in your own house. A placard next to one of the paintings explained that Rembrandt used what was called "impasto," which is thick paint applied heavily to the canvas in such a way that it reflects the light. Sure enough – very thick paint in places. That's just cool.

The Bible also is a work of art, and God has applied excessive amounts of paint in places, to reflect the light. By this I mean that the writers through whom his Spirit breathed the words tended to repeat the words and phrases most important to their message.

Impasto.

So look for the thick places, and you'll appreciate the whole picture of the Bible much better. I do this when I first dive into a book, by reading slowly through it and tallying the "globs" of repeated words. For example, I walked up to the book of Malachi just like I walked up to the Rembrandt painting and started tallying some of the words that I saw repeated. This is what I came up with:

LORD Almighty ///// ///// ///// ///// ///
honor/respect/revere ///// /
pleased ///
accept/////
great ///
name /////////
nations ////
covenant ///// //
curse ///// //
blessed ////
evildoers/wicked/arrogant ///// /

contempt/contemptible ////

defiled //

offerings ///// ///

hands ////

day ///// /

When God breathed his oracle through Malachi, he practically used a shovel-full of paint when it came to the name "LORD Almighty." Even as I could appreciate the Rembrandt impasto and its light-reflecting qualities, it's easy to see Malachi's repeated phrase, applied thick and casting light on God's whole weighty message.

After I made the above list, I stared long at the words used most often. You have to do that with fine art: just sit and look at it. We can almost absorb the entire message of Malachi just from looking at the heavy paint strokes, even without reading the whole sentences in which they're found.

So there ya go – a Bible tip from the National Museum in Amsterdam. Pretty highfalutin', if you ask me.

BIBLE STUDY TIP #32

Ask WHEN.

Do you know what I'm thinking, now that we're at Bible study tip #32? The Bible is a complex piece of literature. In our new culture inundated by social media, we've gotten used to short blog posts and succinct memes, each with a pretty picture, and short videos that give us fast information when we want it. Don't you think it's easy to let that desire for quick information make us impatient with the complexity of Scripture?

I've given you thirty-one tools for approaching the Bible so far, and I'm not done. The Bible is not a simple book. If you've stuck with me this far, I applaud your willingness to be a well-disciplined, hardworking student of the Bible. So are you ready for study tip #32?

Ask WHEN.

You've held the book of Malachi in your hands and have been turning it, to see how it looks on all sides. Let's keep at it. Read the book of Malachi *again*, with a notebook and a pen in hand. This time look for anything that has a time stamp on it and make notes about what you read. Here are a few of my personal notes:

1. *"SINCE the days of your fathers, you have turned from My statues."* (Malachi 3:7a HCSB) Wow, what a long, sad track record for Israel. This one sentence seems to sum up the need for God to bring an oracle.

2. *"NOW we consider the arrogant to be fortunate."* (Malachi 3:15 HCSB) How did Israel come to this sorry conclusion?

3. *"AT THAT TIME those who feared the LORD spoke to one another. The LORD took notice and listened."* (Malachi 3:16a HCSB) So not *all* of Israel has turned away from God. What a hopeful couple of verses.

4. *"They will be Mine,"* says the LORD of Armies, *"a special possession on THE DAY I am preparing."* (Malachi 3:17a HCSB) This verse drips love. I want God to say this about me!

5. *"For indeed, THE DAY is coming, burning like a furnace, when all the arrogant and everyone who commits wickedness will become stubble."* (Mal-

achi 4:1a HCSB) And most of Israel is thinking that the arrogant are fortunate???? What a dangerous oversight. P.S. I do *not* want to be in that burning furnace. P.P.S. Super encouraging that wicked people will get what they deserve. My heart longs for justice in this world.

You guys, are you falling in love with the book of Malachi yet? It's a heavy book, but there's so much rich and even encouraging truth in it. And really we've only looked at it from a few angles.

A closing prayer: May those of us who fear the LORD speak to each other and enjoy God's listening ear. We are his special possession.

As my husband would say, that's very Hallmarky.

BIBLE STUDY TIP #33

Look for imagery.

Matt and I are living with my mother-in-law and her sister now, helpin' out around the place. Our evenings usually begin with *Jeopardy* and *Wheel of Fortune*. Since I'm feeling all game show-ish, how about a little game of our own? Finish these sentences:

> Hungry as a_____.
>
> Quiet as a _____.
>
> Dead as a _____ _.
>
> Slow as _____.
>
> Pretty as a _____.
>
> Dumb as a _____.
>
> Smart as a _____.
>
> Sharp as a _____.

My favorite expression is "dead as a doornail," but that's because of Charles Dickens's wonderful opening page in *A*

Christmas Carol. Here's the second paragraph:

> *Mind! I don't mean to say that I know, of my own knowledge, what there is particularly dead about a doornail. I might have been inclined, myself, to regard a coffin-nail as the deadest piece of ironmongery in the trade. But the wisdom of our ancestors is in the simile; and my unhallowed hands shall not disturb it, or the Country's done for. You will therefore permit me to repeat, emphatically, that Marley was as dead as a doornail.*[3]

We constantly use images in our daily language, to describe more clearly what we're talking about, although not usually with as much brilliance as Dickens. Dickens, however, has nothing on the writers of the Bible for using imagery. Think of David, who describes wanting God so badly that he's "like a deer" panting for water. David isn't really a deer. He's just pulling an image from what he sees around him, to describe how he's feeling in a way that helps us deeply understand what he means.

Let's jump back into Malachi and read a description of the coming of the Lord:

> *But who can endure the day of His coming?*

> *And who will be able to stand when He ap-*
> *pears? For He will be like a refiner's fire and*
> *like cleansing lye. (Malachi 3:2 HCSB)*

See the word repeated twice? *Like.* The Lord will be *like* fire and *like* soap.

Malachi could have just said, "Hey, the Lord's coming, and he's going to purify things." Instead, he uses words like a camera to give us high-resolution photos of a silver refinery and of a laundry room. What is it like to purify things in each of these places? We have to stop and use our imaginations, to see dirty clothes getting scrubbed with a bar of soap or to see a smelter skimming dross off the silver until it is so pure that he can see his own reflection. This is what the coming Messiah will do with the hearts of men.

Images stick in our long-term memories and help us to remember the message attached to them. (That's my schoolteacher side talking.) Images help us to experience truth with our senses. As you open the Bible, look for images that you can save to your mental gallery.

BIBLE STUDY TIP #34

Turn to the Bible for mental health.

How about blunt honesty today? I struggle with severe social anxiety. You wouldn't know it, because I'm super extroverted *with* people, but I'm almost always mentally and emotionally crippled *after* people. I would never tell you this, except that I was chatting with a few young women this summer and they said, "I have that problem, too!"

I'm talking about the hours after I've been in a group of people, when I'm alone in a quiet room or lying in bed. That is when my mind replays every single conversation, and I evaluate and critique all that I said that was probably dumb or offensive or annoying or not cool or dumb or annoying. Probably dumb. Probably annoying. More than likely offensive. It twists my stomach in knots, and I have to work not to groan out loud.

So it was at 1:30 in the morning, after a day of teacher in-service training at school. All the things I said in conversation that day were up for critique, and I was making myself physically ill. But there, in my tossing and turning, the Lord broke in with a verse I knew well:

Cast all your anxiety on him because he cares for you. (1 Peter 5:7)

"Lord," I said, "I am so anxious about my social interactions from today."

He said, "Cast them on me. I care about this part of your life."

To cast means to toss away something that you're holding. I asked the Lord, "Can I really just completely hand over these thoughts and feelings to you?"

His answer was "Yes."

So I did it.

I'm not really sure what the Lord is doing with my inner mess. It wasn't like he said, "Here, hold all of this while I fix it." He just said, "Give it to me." All I know is that after I cast my anxieties into his lap, all I was left holding was the second part of the Bible verse: "he cares for you." I pulled that phrase into my arms like a body pillow, meditating on the sweet truth, and fell into a peaceful sleep.

That brings us to the next Bible study tip: Turn to the Bible for mental health.

It would be interesting to read the Bible from cover to

cover one time, just to take notes from a psychological perspective. There are so many verses about our minds and our thoughts. The Bible talks about depression, anxiety, fear, anger, and pride. It provides a lot of kingdom remedies for whatever ails our thought patterns. Some of the remedies are as simple as, "Hey, toss that mental struggle to me." The Bible shows us that God knows what is happening in our minds, and he cares.

In Isaiah 9:2, we read these words about the coming of Jesus: *"The people walking in darkness have seen a great light."* When I read this, I think about mental darkness and how Jesus comes into our souls, slowly bringing light into all of the corners. Maybe you don't relate to social anxiety, but there's no doubt that you have your own mental struggles.

As you read the Bible, stay alert for verses giving insight and counsel that will improve your mental health. Memorize them, so they become tools you can use in the moment you need them.

BIBLE STUDY TIP #35

Understand covenant.

This summer, our subdivision reworked the homeowner association covenants, so we had to read through them and sign our agreement to the changes. Covenant means that we're not allowed to let the weeds grow up in our front rocks, and we have to keep our garbage cans out of sight. If we don't follow through, we can count on a call from the home association president, because these are rules we all agree to when we move into the neighborhood.

When I pick up the Bible, I see the word *covenant* running as a thread from start to finish, but this is nothing like an HOA covenant.

Would you take a minute and read all of Genesis 15? God comes to Abram and makes him incredible promises of a great reward, to include the possession of the land of Israel and descendants as numerous as the stars. Then God asks Abram to bring a heifer, goat, ram, turtledove, and pigeon.

Except for the birds, Abram cuts them all in half, and lays out each half opposite the other. God comes (in the form of smoking oven and flaming torch) and passes between these animal pieces.

Genesis 15:18 says, *"On that day the LORD made a covenant with Abram..."*

Here's the piece of information that astounded me when I first learned it. Go to blueletterbible.org and look up Genesis 15:18. Then find the original Hebrew definition of the word *made*. It means "cut."

Cut!

The LORD *cut* a covenant with Abram. In doing this, he is saying to Abram, "Do you see these bloody, dead animals that you just *cut* in half? Let the same thing happen to me if I do not keep the promises I have just made to you today."

At this point, I wish I were sitting with the English Bible translators and could say, "Are you kidding me? You want to use the word *made* instead of "*cut* a covenant"? I *made* a covenant with my HOA, but the worst that will happen if I break that covenant with the subdivision is that they'll come spray the weeds in my front rocks and charge me for it.

Cutting covenant is an extreme level of seriousness. It's bloody. In the credits after this story, it should say: "Animals *were* harmed in the making of this covenant."

There are several covenants in the Bible. We see that Noah *cut* covenant with God after the flood. We also see that God *cut* covenant with Moses and the people of Israel. Will you promise me that from now on, when you pick up your Bible and read "*made* a covenant," you'll mentally replace that phrase with "*cut* a covenant"? That one little word changes everything.

Now I challenge you to go read Exodus 24. What very serious agreement is being made and between whom? Then look at what is cut. Pay attention to the blood. This is what it means to understand covenant.

How do you feel, as you think about God's willingness to enter into such serious covenants with men?

BIBLE STUDY TIP #36

Understand the new covenant.

By default, it fell to me, the preacher's wife, to set up the Lord's Supper before our Saturday night worship services. (At your church, you might call it "communion.") I dump little pre-made bread squares into baskets and then fill five silver trays with plastic communion cups. After that, I use a nifty dispenser to fill the tiny cups with grape juice. (I'm Southern Baptist, you guys. None of the hard stuff for us.) When I was little, I could hardly wait until I was allowed to celebrate the Lord's Supper, because who doesn't want a cute little cup of grape juice when your stomach's growling for lunch?

Let's talk about this church tradition: believers breaking bread and sharing the cup (even if it's just Welch's) together. It's all about covenant.

To refresh your memory, our English Bibles talk about people *making* a covenant, but really the original Hebrew word means *cutting* a covenant. An animal is killed, and the person making the covenant essentially says, "If I ever break this solemn promise to you, let what happened to that animal happen to me." There is always bloodshed in a covenant.

Now let's go to the second half of our Bibles: the New Testament, which could be called "the New Covenant." In Hebrews 8:6 we read:

> *But in fact the ministry Jesus has received is as superior to theirs as the covenant of which he is mediator is superior to the old one, since the new covenant is established on better promises.*

This is a comparison between God's covenant with Moses (I hope you read about that last week!) and a new, superior covenant. Jesus is our great high priest, and his ministry is superior to that of the priests who served under the covenant God made with Moses.

As soon as you read about a superior covenant, you should start firing off questions about it:

1. WHAT animal is cut?
2. WHAT parties are involved in the covenant?
3. WHAT are these so-called better promises?

Are you ready for this? Hebrews 9:12 gives us a breath-taking history of our great high priest:

> *He [Christ] did not enter by means of the blood of goats and calves; but he entered the Most Holy Place once for all by his own blood, thus obtaining eternal redemption.*

His own blood, you guys: He was the lamb who was slain, by his own choice. The parties involved in the covenant are God and men. The better promise is that of a permanent redemption and complete cleansing of our consciences.

God cut covenant with all men.

If we believe that Jesus is the lamb who can take away our sins, we get to hear God say, "Let what happened to my Son on the cross happen to me, if I ever break this covenant with you." And we see the blood drip in demonstration of incredible love.

So to me it's never just a plastic cup of Welch's grape juice; it's always a solemn moment to physically remember the covenant. Jesus died for me. The bread represents his body, broken for me. The grape juice represents his blood, spilled for me. This is how I know I am loved.

We cannot be good students of the Bible until we understand covenant and how it has shaped the entire Bible story, from start to finish. Have you entered into this covenant with God?

BIBLE STUDY TIP #37

Eavesdrop wisely.

Toward the end of my junior year of college, I was sitting at a desk waiting for class to start. The guy and girl in front of me were chatting about what minors you could choose in order to get a teaching certificate. As I listened to them, it began to sound like my minor would not allow me to get a teaching certificate, so during the rest of class, I freaked out. Afterwards, I went straight to my English major advisor, who said, "Hmmm, I didn't know that." She sent me to the education director, and there I found out that it was true: I could not get a teaching certificate with a music minor. So in my senior year, I had to add a Spanish minor and an extra semester of college. I'm so glad I eavesdropped in class that day!

Most of what we read in the Bible is one big eavesdropping exercise, but we need to do this carefully.

Let's go to Matthew 28:16-20:

> *Then the eleven disciples went to Galilee, to the mountain where Jesus had told them to go. When they saw him, they worshiped him; but some doubted. Then Jesus came to them and said, "All authority in heaven and on earth has been given to me. Therefore go and make disciples of all nations, baptizing them in the name of the Father and of the Son and of the Holy Spirit, and teaching them to obey everything I have commanded you. And surely I am with you always, to the very end of the age."*

As good Bible students, we immediately start asking questions:

1. WHERE does this scene take place? (A "mountain" in Galilee. You guys, this Montana girl has been to the area of Galilee, and there are only rolling hills. Thus the quotation marks. But to his credit, Matthew had never been to Montana when he wrote this Gospel!)
2. WHEN does this scene take place? (After Jesus was resurrected from the dead.)
3. WHO is there? (The eleven disciples and Jesus.)
4. WHAT commands does Jesus give? (Go, baptize, teach.)

Now let's talk about eavesdropping. Jesus is having an intimate conversation with only eleven people. His commands are for *them*. It is the job of these chosen eleven disciples to go make disciples of all nations. Is the command directed to me? I say no, it has been given to a very specific group of people.

But as an eavesdropper, is there anything that *is* for me? Yes! Here are my thoughts on the takeaway:

Paul tells Timothy (in 2 Timothy 3:16) that all Scripture is God-breathed and useful, so I know that somehow this interaction with Jesus and his disciples is useful for my own life.

In his commands to his eleven disciples, I can hear Jesus' heart. What does he care about? He wants every nation to hear his good news. Jesus wants people to know him and to know the Father. He wants them to be baptized. He wants them to learn how to love him by being obedient to his commands. If Jesus cares so much about the souls in every nation, then as I love Jesus, I'm going to catch that same passion. It's contagious.

When we eavesdrop, we can also back up and look at the whole Bible. Do we see any similar truth in other places? We can return to Malachi and see the same message in God's oracle to Israel:

"My name will be great among the nations, from where the sun rises to where it sets. In every place incense and pure offerings will be brought to me, because my name will be great among the nations," says the Lord Almighty. (Malachi 1:11)

It's impossible to walk closely with God without also starting to care about the nations. If he cares that his name is great in every nation, then we should be asking, "Is there something I can do to help make that happen?" One time a missionary to Africa stayed at our house, and he was so much fun. He taught my little kids to sing songs in Swahili and told us amazing stories. One day he said to me, "You know, I think every believer should have one foot in another country."

Is the command to go, baptize, and teach specifically for us? No, I think it was specifically for the eleven. But the heart behind this command is for every believer. We all should be longing for a way to put one foot in another nation and make God's name great there.

Okay, tell me what nation your foot is in, and how you're investing to make God's name great there.

BIBLE STUDY TIP #38

Know why before you do.

There's hardly a night that I don't wake up at some point anxious about something, and last night was no exception. You're just like me – I know you are. Maybe your worrying happens when you're trying to fall asleep or in the wee hours of the morning, but I know that for most of us, nighttime is when all of the hard things of life surface in our minds. This isn't the first Bible study tip in which I've talked about anxiety, but battling anxiety is a big part of my life, so of course it's going to be a recurring theme in my book. Today's Bible study tip is for what ails us: Know *why* before you *do.*

Let's revisit Peter's simple words to the followers of Jesus: "*Cast all your anxiety on him because he cares for you.*" (*1 Peter 5:7*)

Your shoulders are scrunched and your stomach knotted, maybe because the bills are piling up faster than the money or because a relationship has gone south or because work demands are stressing you out. You look at the command to pitch all your anxiety into God's hands and what is your first reaction?

Maybe you're like me, and your gut reaction is, *If only.* If only it were that easy to toss away all that is causing you an ulcer. But set aside the command for a minute, and think long about the WHY. Why would I take my anxiety and willingly give it to someone else? (Is it that easy?)

There's an important word in this brief verse: *Because.* Talk to us, Peter. Reason with us about how we could live a life free of anxiety. *Because* he cares for you. God cares about all the things that have you tossing and turning in the night. He cares about the outcomes of your finances. He cares about the health of your relationships. He cares about the pressures at work.

He cares about your loneliness.

He cares that you make wise decisions.

He cares about your housekeeping, your yard work, the pile of clean laundry on your bed.

He cares about your desires.

He cares about your health issues.

He cares about your mental struggles.

He cares about your sorrows and tears.

You know what I think? I think we get to the WHY of

casting our cares on God, and we crash head-on into a wall of disbelief. I mean, does anyone really care about us like this? Isn't it a little too good to be true? Someone might ask, "How ya doin'?" but how many who ask really want to hear an answer to that question? And how many people in our lives really want to *do* something about how we're doing? Who actually has the time, energy, and resources to say, "Hey, let me help with that. I really care about what you're going through"?

There's no way to cast your anxiety on the Lord until you've come to grips with the WHY behind the command, which is because God cares for you.

Now think about every time you open your Bible and see a command to do something. Before you even consider obeying, will you search out the reasoning behind the command and give it careful consideration? You might find that if you truly embrace the WHY, then the DO will naturally follow without much effort.

And hey, let's believe God means what he says, eh? He really cares about all our stuff, in a "give it to me" sort of way.

BIBLE STUDY TIP #39

Memorize truth about life and death.

Hard day for me today. I received one of those wee-hour phone calls, with the news that my sweet aunt had slipped away from us in the night. She had suffered many long, painful months from cancer. As I lay in bed, trying to absorb the idea of her not being with us anymore, Bible truth came to my mind in quiet but powerful waves, redirecting my thinking and giving me hope and joy.

When my dad abruptly and unexpectedly went to be with the Lord over four years ago, I remember the shock of worship in church every week after that. Even though I grew up in the church, I never realized how much we sing about death and life. That is just weird. Don't you think it's weird?

We sing about Jesus' blood and the cross and our own hope of resurrection, and when we sing about being alive forever in heaven with Jesus, the music turns celebratory and upbeat. But that hopefulness is always mixed with the message that, "Hey, you're gonna die. We're all gonna die." Maybe it's not until you lose someone you love that you pick up your Bible and truly see the message of eternity throughout, but we need to think long and hard on these truths about death and life.

Paul talks about this topic as a matter of fact:

> *For to me, to live is Christ and to die is gain. If I am to go on living in the body, this will mean fruitful labor for me. Yet what shall I choose? I do not know! I am torn between the two: I desire to depart and be with Christ, which is better by far. (Philippians 1:21-23)*

Who talks like that???

Yet these are the words that came to my mind at 4:30 in the morning, after the phone call about my aunt jolted us out of a sound sleep: "To die is gain." So I lay there and meditated on this verse I had memorized years ago, considering the fact that my aunt's death was nothing but gain for her. She gained a new body, complete freedom from sin, and a face-to-face with her Savior. This was of great comfort to me.

On a practical note, I want to tell you that when someone you love dies, that's not the time for you to say, "Oh,

I think I need to do a Bible study about this." No, you're going to be going through a box of Kleenex, making plans for a funeral and grieving all the 1,037 things you're going to miss about that person. (Who will make paper-thin sugar cookies for us this Christmas, if not Aunt Karyn?) In the middle of this sorrow and stress, you do not have time for a deep Bible study.

You need to store up God's word in your mind and heart on a daily basis.

Now let me go all school-teacher on you and tell you that everybody can learn, and nobody's brain ever exploded from putting in some mental labor. I see that look on your face that tells me, "But I just can't memorize things!" I'm giving you teacher eyes that say, "Yes, you can. Suck it up and do the work." (Can I say, "Suck it up?")

When hard news of any flavor hits, you need truth and you need it *now*. You need to know what the Bible says about death and catastrophe and sickness. You need an arsenal of hopeful statements to combat all of the fear, doubts, anger, and hopelessness that threaten to take your legs out from under you. There's so much good stuff in the Bible about death, which is why we sing about it at church. The Bible shouts hope and life and joy into your darkest day.

Here's how it goes: you get a note card and write a verse on it that speaks hopeful, truthful words about death and life. Then every day you say the verse until you can do it from memory. Think about it. Pray about it. Cram it into your brain and then recall, recall, recall until you can say it by heart. And honestly? You might think that doing some big, fancy Bible study is what good Christians do, but memorizing small truths one at a time is the richest, most life-changing investment you can make.

Start with Philippians 1:21. It's short.

BIBLE STUDY TIP #40

Learn from contrasting examples.

A few days ago I went to a funeral home in Wyoming, for a family viewing of my aunt. Well, a viewing of my aunt's dead body. (How else could I say it?) There were a lot of tears that evening, as we tried to absorb the fact that she was gone from us. For me, the thought of not hearing her voice say, "Hey Chris," cut me deeply.

But the family and many friends were there for an hour, and during that time we also laughed and hugged and encouraged each other a lot. As we were leaving, I wondered about the funeral director who sat in his office just around the corner, with an open door. He must hear a lot of different kinds of grieving come from the parlor. From us he heard sadness mixed with a boatload of hope and joy. The majority of my family follows Christ, and we listened to this one instruction from Paul:

Brothers and sisters, we do not want you to be

*uninformed about those who sleep in death,
so that you do not grieve like the rest of man-
kind, who have no hope. For we believe that
Jesus died and rose again, and so we believe
that God will bring with Jesus those who have
fallen asleep in him. (1 Thessalonians 4:13-14)*

See? I told you the Bible is packed full of death and life information. I hope you'll add Paul's words to your Bible memory list, because you will need them someday.

Let's consider Paul's contrasting examples. He points to "the rest of men" (those who refuse to believe in Jesus' glorious resurrection) and says, "Do you see how those people grieve? Can you hear them during the viewing, as they hopelessly sob and wail beside the casket? Don't grieve like them. Don't be ignorant about death like they are." (Here I add another shameless plug for you to memorize verses about death and life. That's the antidote to ignorance.)

I bet the funeral director can tell in a matter of minutes what kind of people he has in his parlor, whether they're normal men who have no answers for the pain that has come into their lives, or whether they're followers of Christ who are filled with a confident anticipation of seeing their loved one again. Surely it's a stark contrast.

As I come back into my regular routine, after celebrating the beautiful life of my aunt, I look back on her funeral weekend as a very sweet time. We felt the squeeze of grief often, to be sure, but we know Aunt Karyn is alive in Christ. It's just a few sleeps of our own and then we'll see her again. Hope wins.

The Bible is filled with contrasts, which means that two very different things are displayed side by side. As we look at the two, we are forced to make a decision of one over the other. Keep your eyes open for these contrasts as you're reading, and choose the better life.

When you consider or encounter death, will you choose to live in ignorance and despair or knowledge and hope?

BIBLE STUDY TIP #41

Zoom out.

The other night, I was teaching the kids at church, and their Bible verse was a very uplifting, beautiful verse that describes who God is. I could hardly wait to teach it to them. Here, read it for yourself:

> *He is the Rock, his works are perfect, and all his ways are just. A faithful God who does no wrong, upright and just is he. (Deuteronomy 32:4)*

Isn't that lovely?

Yeah, until I decided to sip my morning coffee and read *around* the verse to get a feel for the context. I zoomed out, to the beginning of Deuteronomy 31, where I read the back story that made me cringe and then made me cry.

In Deuteronomy 31, the children of Israel were about to take over their new Promised Land, which sounds well and good. Except that God knew, before his chosen people ever dipped their toes into the Jordan River, that when they got into their new land they would abandon him and worship false gods. So he made Moses teach them a song.

Fun! A song, you think. But the song goes something like this, if you'll allow me to paraphrase:

> God is the Rock, his works are perfect.
> But Israel has ditched him.
> Seriously?
> After all he's done for them?
> Now they're worshiping gods
> that used to freak them out.
> New gods with no track record.
> Busted. God saw all this.
> They were totally clueless,
> and the LORD rejected them.
> Let the record show:
> He is the only god.

Okay, so that's the gist. (Umm, you might want to read it for yourself: Deuteronomy 32.) The Israelites had to learn this song. They had to sing it over and over again, *before* they went into the Promised Land, so that when the Lord's punishment came on them later, they would be like, "Wait, this sounds like that song we used to know. How did it go again?" And they would sing it together from memory. Deuteronomy 31:19 says, *"So that it may be a witness for me against them."* Can you imagine learning a song about your coming failure? That's why I cried for them.

The children's memory verse I was teaching on Wednesday night turned out to be lyrics from a "This is why you're in trouble" song. Once we knew that, it really changed the tone of voice in which we recited it together. If I had just read that memory verse by itself, I probably would have taught the kids about how awesome God is. But once I learned the context, my lesson changed to a sober lesson for *us*. It was a lesson that we had better remember who the one and only God is.

So always zoom out, you guys. Never, ever just read one verse and think you've got it all figured out. Take time to read the verses around it. Better than that, read the chapters around it. Better than that, read the book around it.

The greater context directs the meaning of the smaller parts.

Oh, and by the way: God was faithful to punish his wayward children, but he was also faithful to love them. He even sent Jesus to take the punishment for all of their failures. Thinking about that made me cry a different kind of tears.

God loves us, even when we're naughty.

BIBLE STUDY TIP #42

Follow the path to Jesus.

We were just watching *Finding Nemo* in my Spanish class, from which movie comes this profound truth: All drains lead to the ocean. You're going to have to forgive me for this, but that thought inspired today's Bible tip: All Scripture leads to Jesus.

You pick up this thick book, the Holy Bible, and it's totally intimidating. But it's a lot less scary if you think of the whole thing as an introduction to Jesus. I'm picturing the Father of the bride gently grasping his daughter's hand and placing it into the hand of her groom.

The Bible is the poignant handoff. Give God your hand, and as you turn the pages of the Bible, imagine him giving you to the Son, to belong to him forever and ever. This is everything you've been waiting for: to be loved and cared for by someone who delights in you. All of the words in this big book are to bring you into the relationship where you'll be cherished for eternity.

The writer of Hebrews shows us how to look for Jesus in all of Scripture. For example, he says that Moses was faithful in God's house, but Jesus built the house (see Hebrews 3:1-6). He talks about the high priests in the Old Testament and then describes Jesus as the *great* high priest (see Hebrews 4:14-15). He talks about the priest Melchizedek and how Jesus is unique like he was (see Hebrews 7).

But the best pointing toward Jesus is to look at God's covenant with Moses, and see how Jesus ushered in a new covenant. (That's why we have two parts of the Bible: old and new covenants.) Consider this:

> *But when Christ came as high priest of the good things that are now already here, he went through the greater and more perfect tabernacle that is not made with human hands, that is to say, is not a part of this creation. He did not enter by means of the blood of goats and calves; but he entered the Most Holy Place once for all by his own blood, thus obtaining eternal redemption. (Hebrews 9:11-12)*

All through the Old Testament, we see the Israelite priests making sacrifices to atone for the sins of the people. But Jesus came, as the great high priest, and *cut* covenant with us. He became the perfect sacrifice, the last sacrifice ever needed. His blood was enough, wonderfully enough, to cover all of our sins forever.

Do you remember when Moses was helping the Israelites escape slavery in Egypt? The night before their escape, each family killed a lamb and put the blood on the doorposts. The angel of death passed over their houses because of this. This story points to Jesus. Do you see it?

Jesus is the lamb.

Jesus is the sacrifice.

When we put all of our hope and trust in Jesus, death passes over us.

So when you pick up the Bible, always ask, "How does this story put my hand into the hand of Jesus?" For all that is difficult to understand or confusing in the Bible, always remember that the main point of the book is just to help you come into relationship with God, through the sacrifice of Jesus his Son.

I'd like you to do something. There's a Bible written for preschoolers, which I mentioned in study tip #19, and it powerfully shows how the entire Bible leads us to Jesus. It's called *The Jesus Storybook Bible: Every Story Whispers His Name*, by Sally Lloyd-Jones. (Stop and think about that title for just a minute!) Every adult should read this book at least once. Think of it as the most delightful, easy-to-read seminary textbook you'll ever pick up. You could buy it to read for yourself and then give it to a child.

Have you placed your hand in the hand of Jesus?

BIBLE STUDY TIP #43

Ten ways to experience closeness with God when you open your Bible.

A while ago, someone asked me, "What if I don't emotionally connect with God when I read the Bible?" It's a great question, because we don't want to approach the Bible like it's a textbook. We want our hearts to be transformed. We want to come away feeling loved – deeply loved. We want to experience nearness to God.

But how to make that happen?

In high school, when I first started opening my Bible as a daily habit, it was kind of a miracle if I could stick with it for five minutes. It felt mechanical, like a chore. The first day that began to change is vivid in my mind. I was sitting on my tall bed, with its very old green iron frame. My Bible was open in front of me, and I realized that God had answered a very specific prayer I had prayed. I wish I had written down the details, because I don't remember what

I had asked God for or how he answered it. I just remember thinking, *Oh my word, God was actually listening to me.* That day was the beginning of a feeling of closeness to God as I studied the Bible. It didn't completely flip a switch forever, but it was a taste of intimacy that slowly grew into a permanent experience.

So let's see if I can turn this into a list, because what you want is a specific instruction to help you get to that same place. Here's my best attempt to deconstruct my own experience:

1. Study the Bible as a discipline. God wants to be close to you, so just keep at it. If it feels like a discipline, *that's okay.* Very normal, you guys! I imagine that very few people decide to follow Christ and then – bam – immediately arrive at an intimate friendship.

2. Believe and obey. Jesus tells us that obedience is our expression of love for God, so as you believe and act on what you read, it is going to fuel the fire of relationship. God is going to be smiling at you!

3. Wait. Do you know how many times the Bible tells us to wait on the Lord? A kajillion. If you feel like you're waiting for a close feeling with

him, well, yeah. There's something special about waiting for him to reveal himself. It conveys to him that you want relationship with him. You're hungry for him. You're stubbornly hanging out in his word until he shows up. Waiting doesn't mean there's something wrong with you! It's just part of what it means to follow God. Again: very normal and even something we're instructed to do. How long will you have to wait before you feel close to God? I have no idea. You're welcome.

4. Any relationship is damaged by sin, and for sure you're not going to feel close to God, if you're continuing willfully in a sin. So daily confess and turn away from your sin.

5. Don't pull away in hurt and disappointment. Feeling distant from God might make you want to throw your hands up and yell, "Fine, forget it! I'll just do life on my own." But James 4:8 says, *"Come near to God and he will come near to you."* Do you want God to come near? Then you *have to* keep coming near to him, for as long as it takes until he comes near to you. Withdrawing from a relationship never makes it better.

6. Trust that he will come close. Again, James 4:8

makes this huge promise: *"He will come near to you."* He will! While you're waiting, hold onto this promise with a death grip. You can pray (day after day), "Lord, you promise to come near to me. I'm waiting on that. I want that with all my heart."

7. Humble yourself. God really hates pride. When you are willing to admit how needy and sinful you are, that's going to open up the door of relationship. If you're pridefully trying to live life on your own power, you're communicating to God that you don't need him. Relationship killer. If you're pridefully living in anxiety, trying to manipulate your own future and make it want you want it to be, you're telling God that you have your future under control and don't need him. Relationship killer. If you're unwilling to admit you have dark places in your heart, you're telling God you don't need Jesus – you don't need a Savior. Relationship killer. Human pride and intimacy with God cannot coexist.

8. Give thanks. This is super important, because God wants you to see all the good he's doing in your life. The more you notice all of his daily good gifts, big and small, the more you're saying

to him, "I see you." Honestly, it's a little flirty. It's that look across the room that says, "Hey, I know we're in a crowd of people, but I see you over there, and I like what I see." Believe me, I live in a Hallmark Channel house, and do you know what Hallmark's got that we all love so much? The look. Two people exchanging a long look. Do you see God in your day? Or are you just thinking about him for the five minutes when you're studying the Bible? That's not going to cut it. He wants *you* – all day long. He wants to know you're thinking about him and seeing how wonderful he is, in every situation.

9. Pray for every little thing you need, and look for God's provision. Like I said, things changed for me when I saw God answering my specific prayers. He's listening to you! He wants to take care of you, and the more details of your life in which you ask him for help, the more you're going to see him at work. You'll start to feel loved and cared for. You'll start to see how incredibly creative and resourceful he is.

10. Go to church and worship with other believers. If you're trying to know God all by yourself, without going to church and without worship-

ing with other believers, you're going to be disappointed. God has specifically gifted each person in the church so that we see different shades of who God is when we get together. Also, as we sing praises to the Lord and hear the Bible preached, it adds layers to our relationship with God that we just can't get in a daily quiet time all by ourselves. Even though church is flawed (because of the people), it is still God's tool for helping you get to know him.

Okay, so there you go. If you look at the above list, you can see that having a close relationship with God is complex. Good things that are complex in this life are worth the effort, worth the time, and worth the perseverance. Stick with it, friend.

BIBLE STUDY TIP #44

Get familiar with God's voice.

A while back I put up my fall decorations, which makes me feel happy on the inside. My mom has been the main benefactor in giving me this earthy, warm decor, so I took a selfie in front of some of my pumpkins and texted it to her.

"Thanks for giving me all of these beautiful decorations, Mom!" I said.

"Those don't even look like pumpkins," she responded.

What? I stared at the text. This wasn't what I expecting from my mom. She's the kind, quiet librarian lady who only ever says nice things. It kind of hurt my feelings. Maybe she was joking?

"Yes, they do!" I sent back. (Keeping it playful?)

"They look like pincushions with some dead leaves behind them," she said.

Oh, seriously? I texted back with screaming exclamation points, "Arie!!!!!!!"

"Hey sis," he replied. "Mom and I are in the car on our way to Casper. She's driving and can't text right now."

Two sentences, you guys. It only took me two sentences to realize it was my brother's snotty voice I was reading in the texts instead of Mom's *nice* one. I've heard him rant about all of our junky decorations for years. (We ignore him, by the way.)

People have a certain voice, you know. This is one of the first things you learn when you become a writer. "Develop your own voice," the experts say. That means you have this way of expressing yourself on paper that people can hear and feel, in your word choices and sentence construction and rhythm. Some people use a soothing, quiet voice. Some use a poetic voice with "swirly words," as my friend describes it. Some people, like me, just kind of bark out truth with a hey-you-should-listen-to-me kind of tone. (I sound just like my dad, if you care to know.)

Jesus has a voice. He says this to his followers: *"My sheep listen to my voice; I know them, and they follow me." (John 10:27)*

Disciplined Bible study means you become familiar with the voice of God, which is interesting considering the fact that over thirty different men penned the Scriptures. The words were breathed into them by the Spirit of God, however, and if you start at the beginning and read to the end, you start to hear the lilt of God's voice. You start to identify his word choices. The passions of his heart start to rise to the surface, so that you're less and less surprised when he keeps talking about the same themes.

Familiarity takes time, though. If I were to hand you a book, written by an author you hadn't read, you wouldn't be able to read just one or two sentences from the book and say, "I know this person's voice now." You would have to read the whole thing. You would have to read the happy chapters and the scary chapters and the hard chapters, to get a feel for the continuity of voice in different settings.

So what I'm saying to you is, "Keep studying! Keep reading!" (See? My barky voice.) Every time you make the effort to open your Bible, you're training your ear to hear the voice of God.

The voice that created the world.

The voice that quiets storms.

The voice that drives out demons.

The voice that raises the dead.

The voice that says, "You are mine, and I am taking care of you."

It's a voice that has the power to change everything in your life, so you need to listen, listen, listen, until Jesus' voice becomes so familiar you could recognize it even as a whisper in your ear.

BIBLE STUDY TIP #45

#nofilter

It was in the basement of our old church, all the way down the hall and around the corner, when someone first challenged my view of the creation story in Genesis. A bunch of us young married couples smooshed into this windowless room for Sunday school every week and grew deep in our knowledge of the Bible.

"God created the world in six days – six literal days," said the teacher.

But my public school upbringing had draped a fabric of *evolution* over my eyes, so I had always looked through that fabric when I read the creation story. Of course. I mean, absolutely of course I believed God made the earth and everything in it, but "six days" probably was symbolic for the time it took for all of these things to evolve. Right?

Except that our teacher said, "No. Six *days*."

This was a jolt to my belief system, but I gave it thought

and reconsidered my stance on creation. I bravely looked at the words in the Bible without my preconceived beliefs.

I'm not writing this to debate creation versus evolution, but I want to urge you not to use a filter when you read the Bible. When I say "filter," I mean all of the presuppositions with which you approach the Bible. All the stuff your grandma and mom and dad told you when you were growing up. All the stuff your church teachers or pastors told you. All the stuff you learned in school or read in a magazine or studied in a book or saw in a meme on Facebook. All of these influences (truthful or untruthful) have shaped your thinking over the years, and you have to be super careful not to let them drape over your eyes when you read the Scripture.

If you're on Instagram, you know that you can call up your *real* picture and then change the filter that goes over the picture. You can take your *real* picture and cover it with "Gingham" or "Moon" or "Inkwell."Pretty soon, you have a photo that looks good, but it isn't authentic anymore.

Sometimes we like to read the Bible and cover it with the "What-I-Want-To-Hear" filter.

Probably one of the most terrifying things to do, when you read the Bible, is to say, "Okay, Lord, what are you saying to me in this passage of Scripture?" There's a good chance that he might say something you don't want to hear.

Maybe he'll say something that goes against what you always thought when you were growing up. Maybe he'll ask you to do things you do not want to do, or go places you do not want to go.

Risk.

It's a risk to read with no filter and let the Lord say what he wants to say. But it's also where the Kingdom adventure is. Will you stay safe or follow the King?

Take the risk; ask to see the naked truth on the page.

BIBLE STUDY TIP #46

Delight in the Bible when you're awake.

I'm one of those annoying morning people who bounces out of bed ready to conquer the world. I eat first breakfast at 5:00 and second breakfast around 9:00. Much of my important work for the day is often accomplished before many of you have turned off your alarm clock. So you might be afraid that I'm going to tell you to study the Bible in the first minutes after you wake up. But my answer is more challenging than that. Brace yourself: Study the Bible when you're awake.

You night owls are saying, "Sweet. So around 11:00 in the morning, then?"

And I say, "No, when you are awake. The *whole* time you are awake."

The Psalmist sings about a man who prospers, like a healthy tree that produces a lot of fruit: "*Whose delight is in the law of the LORD, and who meditates on his law day and night."(Psalm 1:2)*

We've been talking about studying the Bible in different ways, but the psalmist gives us a replacement for the word *study*. He uses the word *delight*. I'm not sure if you have ever used that word when it comes to opening up your Bible. *Study* might be a synonym for drudgery, but *delight* means you sneak into something at every possible moment.

You delight in the hot chocolate chip cookies, so you keep having "just one more."

You delight in your new fuzzy sweatshirt, so you keep slipping into it, every time it comes out of the dryer.

You delight in a new book, so you read it under the covers with a flashlight when you should be going to sleep.

I'm a teacher, you know, and at the beginning of the year I always talk to my students about work ethic. I let them know that there are many students who work very, very hard *to do the least amount of work possible.* Can you hear me saying that to you about Bible study? Do you want me to tell you when it's the optimum time to study the Bible, so that you can do just a little bit, the smallest amount, and it will last you a long time? Sorry.

People who delight in the word of God are always asking, "How can I find times to slip away with the Lord, all day long?"

Delight means you read your Bible in the morning. You

hang a memory verse at your desk, to think about during the day. You follow people on social media who speak Bible truth and un-follow all the rest. You listen to gospel-centered worship music while you're driving. You think and pray about your morning Bible reading while you're folding socks. You read a verse before you start dinner. You look up the meaning of a word, because you just have to understand what it is you're studying. You roll a memory verse around in your mind while you're drifting off to sleep.

Delight means you're never happy with just a little. Instead of asking, "Did I do enough?" you're asking, "How can I do more?"

You can start now by spending an hour looking carefully at your whole daily schedule. How can you insert the Bible into all of your activities? It could be as easy as writing a memory verse on several note cards and planting the cards along your daily path. (If you stop to look at these and meditate on them during the day, that counts as Bible study.)

Someone was just asking me how to create a lifestyle like I've described, and I told her that it is simply work. You work to delight in the word of God. (Is that possible? To work to delight in something? I say yes.) Think. Plan. Decide. Because you want to be a person who is like a tree that always has green, healthy leaves and is loaded with fruit. That means you need to work towards a lifestyle of meditating on God's word day and night.

Delight will be the unavoidable outcome.

BIBLE STUDY TIP #47

Employ the open-and-point method.

Sometimes I do a deep Bible study, where I'm looking up Greek word meanings and asking a lot of questions and researching historical information and doing serious cross-referencing.

And sometimes not. Sometimes I'm just downing a bowl of Frosted Mini-Wheats and I want to read the Bible for a second. So I open to one of three tried-and-true places, swirl my pointer finger in a circle, and plop it down on a verse. Voila. Instant Bible study. Eat a bite of cereal. Read the verse. Think about it. Respond to it in prayer. Rinse out the cereal bowl. Hop into the shower.

Yeah, it can be that simple. (Why do we like to make things really, really hard?)

My three go-to places are the Psalms, Proverbs, and the four Gospels. I like these books, because they're not usually super complicated to understand. They're real-life. And usually you can read a few verses from these places and get a complete thought. (Although never allow yourself to read a verse without thinking of its context. Never, ever!)

I like the Psalms, because the writers are so *real*. They talk about being depressed and feeling hopeless and wondering where God is and how long before he shows up. It's always nice to hear from authentic people.

I like the Proverbs, because they're so straightforward. King Solomon says, "Live like this." Okay, then.

I like the Gospels, because all hope is in Jesus. Hanging out with him while you eat your cereal can be enough to change the whole course of your day. The Gospels are where we're reminded that we're sinners (which is actually encouraging), and where God says, "I love you. See? Sending my Son to fix everything." The Gospels are where we get our heads on straight about what Kingdom life means. A good place to start the day.

So there you have it: Christy Fitzwater's amazing, never-before-seen Bible study method: Open. Point. Read.

Doesn't have to be complicated, you guys.

BIBLE STUDY TIP #48

Read the Bible through.

When I was in middle school, our pastor challenged us to read the Bible through in a year, and I did. #spiritualnerd

Several years ago, I asked for *The One-Year Bible* and decided to read the whole Bible again in a year. This time it took me four years to accomplish the task. At one point, I was so off on the calendar days at the top of each page that I almost gave up. But then I didn't. I just kept plugging away. Slow and steady wins the race.

My favorite way to study the Bible is to land in one place and spend a whole week looking at just a few verses. This would be my highest recommendation for you. But I think everyone should read the Bible from cover-to-cover at least once or twice in his or her lifetime.

Genesis to Revelation. One page at a time. One book at a time.

Why? Because the Bible tells one story. It's one long,

colorful, scary, suspenseful history lesson about how God made the world and then we messed it up and then he swept in for the rescue. Good overcomes evil. Heroes and villains. Nail-biting climax. All seems lost. Exciting conclusion. Bad guy gets what's coming to him. Happily ever after.

You definitely need to read the whole thing.

And don't give up when you get to Leviticus. Leviticus is the quicksand that sucks under many a well-intentioned Bible reader, but stand your ground. All the way through Leviticus, think about the coming of Jesus.

And no skipping over genealogy lists. They matter. You can read them word-for-word at least once in your life.

There are so many ways to read the whole Bible. You can buy a special Bible that has the Scripture apportioned into 365 days. Or you can go online and download any number of reading plans that you can cross off as you go along.

May I suggest an amazing app I recently discovered? Check out The Bible Project, and you will be delighted. These guys have made short but masterful animated synopsis videos of each book of the Bible, which you can watch on their app. You can also do your daily Bible reading on the app, and it keeps track of where you are. My two favorite things about this are that the app travels with you on your phone, so you can do a little reading while you're out and about. Also, in the app they've placed these lovely quiet spaces where you focus your heart and mind before reading. (You have to see it to believe it.) If you like technology, this is an excellent choice.

Remember I said that you always want to consider context when you read verses from the Bible? The best way to do this is to become familiar with the entire Bible. There's no shortcut for this except to buckle down and read it from start to finish in a year (or in one "dog year" as I did.)

My aunt recently went to be with Jesus, you know, and we celebrated the fact that she read the whole Bible *every year*. Wow. If she can do that, you can at least read it through once, eh? You can do it!

BIBLE STUDY TIP #49

Read out loud.

Do you know that my mom is a children's librarian? She has invested hours of her life reading out loud to children in her community and just as many hours reading out loud to grandkids sitting next to her in the wing-backed chair by the fireplace. So we know how to read out loud at our house, with all of the voices and sound effects that come with a good children's book.

My grandma used to read out loud to us, too. After making us a feast for breakfast, which included homemade butter spread thick on homemade waffles, with crisp bacon, whole milk straight from the farm, and two different kinds of juice, she would pull out her Bible, which weighed almost as much as she did, and put on her reading glasses. While I finished my grape juice, she would read a Bible story. I especially remember the story of Abram moving when God told him to move, except that her version included semi-trucks.

"Grandma!" I said. "Semi-trucks?"

"Just wanted to see if you were payin' attention," she said.

There's something special about reading out loud, and I wonder if you've tried that in your Bible study time. We have a Youth With a Mission base near us, and those students spend nine months studying several times through every book of the Bible. With each book, one of their homework assignments is to sit down with a few other students and read it out loud to one another.

Reading out loud has several practical benefits. First, it gives you the opportunity to read the Bible as story. Words can be awfully flat and mechanical on the page, but when we speak them we can employ special emphasis. We can use our imaginations and make characters and dialogue come to life. We can add suspenseful or mournful or angry or loving tones. There have been times that I've read a truth out loud and then have wept upon hearing the beauty of it.

Reading out loud is also very slow work, and slow is good when it comes to understanding the Bible. I can skim a page of text with my eyes and miss half of the details, but you can't "skim" out loud. Reading aloud means speaking every single word and taking time to breathe in between phrases. The slow read can lead to better understanding.

Letting Bible truths roll off of our tongues also has a benefit for long-term memory. The more of our body and senses we use in learning information, the more likely it is that the information will stick in our brains.

So maybe give reading out loud a go sometime? There are so many benefits. It might feel like a strange exercise at first, but it also might wake up your heart and mind to new wonders in God's word.

BIBLE STUDY TIP #50

Grab a pen.

Okay, we teachers know that students need to write and write and write. In the interaction between your eyes and your hand and the paper, something happens in your brain that helps you mentally process and retain information.

So writing should be a part of Bible study.

But I have to tell you that I do *not* write in my Bible. Not that I think there's anything wrong with it, but every time I open the Bible I want it to be as if for the first time. I don't want any old stuff crowding what God might want to teach me today.

I do write, though. For me it's 3x5 cards. If you ever can't think what to buy me for my birthday, you can buy me 3x5 cards. White. Ruled. Save your money on the diamonds, because I don't find them as valuable. On these cards, I write down verses and any thought I want to remember. Often I stick them in places where I'll see and think about the information again.

You could use your Bible as a remembering place. There's something extremely valuable about a Bible that's filled with personal notes. Use those lovely margins to write notes about what God is teaching you as you read. Then the next time you go to that place, you can remember his goodness. God loves it when we remember what he's done and the lessons he has taught us, and these little notes you leave for yourself might be bricks for your future faith.

Or how about a journal? Those 50-cent composition journals are my favorite. I've scribbled up a bunch of those with lessons from the Lord, verses I've had questions about, and truths I never, ever want to forget. Not too long ago, I came across one of those notebooks when I was cleaning out a drawer, and I sat and read through it for a long time. There it was on the page: proof that God had been working in my life and growing me. The pages were filled with verses that had given me direction in times of change, and in seasons of pain and questioning.

My husband likes to write dates in his Bible, so he knows when he studied a passage last. That's not a bad idea. (Except for me, because I just can't do it! Just can't write in my Bible. But whatevs.)

What matters, though, is that you don't just read truth but also write it. Let the information come through your eyes and swirl around in your brain and mark itself on paper through your fingers. This will make a difference in how well you absorb the truth of God's words.

Write, write, write.

BIBLE STUDY TIP #51

Consult outside resources.

I gave an assignment to my Spanish students: fill in a verb study guide and then come get my key to check if they were correct. Not long after handing out the pages, I looked over and saw that one of the students had grabbed the key and was filling in her study guide.

"Yeah, I don't think so," I said, as I took away the key.

"Whaaaat?" she said. Because the guilty always say "What?" as if they can't possibly understand why they're in trouble.

"Do the work first. Think. *Then* come and get the key and check your work," I said.

Let's admit, en masse, that we're all fairly lazy and would rather someone else do the work and just hand it to us. We certainly have this propensity when it comes to Bible study. But I've given you fifty ideas so far, to help *you* do the work. You think. You study. You ask questions and look for key words and consider context and do some cross-referencing.

Then, and only then, grab outside "keys" and check your work.

The person who does the heavy lifting, when it comes to Bible study, is the one who learns the most and grows the most. You want to be that person. When you dig and do hard work and spend time in God's word, it impacts you in a way that you will never experience just being spoon-fed by someone else.

I use a lot of outside helps, such as reading devotional books, listening to sermons, and consulting Bible commentaries. But these are only a supplement to the hard work I've already done. When I read a commentary, I can hold the author's educated opinion up to my own educated opinion. I gather facts and interpret the Scripture for myself *first*, before listening to the voices of others. Then I can discern whether the outside voice is spot-on or not.

The danger with outside voices is that sometimes they're wrong. We need to be good students, so that we can tell if a teacher is wrong or not. In Acts 17:11, we see an excellent example set by the people of Berea, with whom Paul and Silas shared the message of Jesus:

Now the Bereans were of more noble character

than the Thessalonians, for they received the message with great eagerness and examined the Scriptures every day to see if what Paul said was true.

Let's talk about the beauty of noble character as it pertains to Bible study. Here noble character means that you don't just listen to some preacher or author or professor and swallow what they're saying. You hold a little bit of healthy skepticism, until you've done your own homework in the Bible and can confirm that the outside voice is speaking the truth.

I do encourage you to listen to outside voices, because often a Bible scholar can help you understand Scripture in a new way or can explain something you couldn't otherwise understand. But make sure that the person you listen to focuses on Jesus and the gospel. This is always the test.

Jesus and the gospel: God's creation of the world, our sinful fall, our need for a Savior, and Jesus' divine rescue. If a speaker or author doesn't stay centered on these facts, then don't listen to that person. The gospel is the center of the whole Bible, and there is *danger*danger*danger*danger* if anyone veers away from these simple truths. Be very careful to whom you listen.

Do your own homework before consulting a key.

BIBLE STUDY TIP #52

Add faith.

You have stuck with me for a long time! If you've made it this far, I applaud your heart that longs to know how to read and understand God's word for yourself. Longing for God is a good start to knowing him.

I'd like to end with a final word from the book of Hebrews. The writer (we don't know who he is) reminds the Jews of what happened when they wandered in the wilderness. They hardened their hearts against believing God's instruction that they could enter the Promised Land and conquer it. Because of this hardening of hearts, that generation died in the wilderness and never got to enter into Israel.

In Hebrews 4:2, we read:

> *For we also have had the gospel proclaimed to us, just as they did; but the message they heard was of no value to them, because they*

did not share the faith of those who obeyed it.

It's possible for you to follow all of my Bible study tips and still find the Bible to be of no value to you. I hope that freaks you out.

If you study the Bible diligently but don't combine what you read with faith, then you might as well throw all of your work in the garbage. I teach at a private Christian school, so I know very well that students can study the Bible, memorize huge chunks of it, write essays about it, present the words in speeches, and still walk away with hard hearts that don't believe a word of it. Studying doesn't equal heart transformation. Only those who add faith to their Bible knowledge come out of our school knowing God.

If you want to enter into the "Promised Land," you have to combine your study with faith. When you gather facts and begin to understand what you're reading, you have to decide every time whether you're going to believe it and obey it. Are the words of the Bible true? Then they should transform your entire way of thinking and your lifestyle. This is the evidence that you have had faith in what you've read.

I highly recommend that you be a little afraid when you pick up your Bible – a little terrified of what truth you'll encounter, to which you're going to have to bend your knees.

If you go in ready to combine faith with what you see on the page, you are going to have to change. And all God's people said?

Ugh.

But it's an adventure! Come on, you want adventure. You want transformation and the hard-but-meaningful trail, not the easy, don't-mess-with-me path.

How can I better explain to you the importance of faith and its connection to Bible study? My thoughts go to when my daughter was born and a lady gave me a few hourglass-shaped flannel things. *Hmmmm,* I thought, as I said, "Thank you" to the gift giver with all sincerity but complete ignorance. I had no idea what those flannel things were, until one day a month or so later, when she approached me at church and said, "How are you liking the burp rags?" *Burp rags!*

"They're wonderful," I said.

Except they had been stuck in the back of a drawer for weeks, and I didn't actually *know* they were wonderful until I went home, pulled them out, and started using them all the time. They were just perfect to throw over the shoulder, protect my shirt sleeve from baby spit-up, and then toss in the wash.

Bible study without faith is like burp rags tucked in a back drawer. The truth of Scripture needs to be pulled out and worn out. It's meant to be used in real, messy life situations. Only then will you know how beautiful and powerful this book really is.

So as I come to the end of these study tips, my hope is that you can now open your Bible and feel like, *Hey, I can figure out this message all by myself!* As you understand the Bible, I want to hear you say you're believing what you're understanding and that believing is changing your whole life. In the end, may you joyfully declare, "Now I know God in a way I've never experienced before." May the Lord show you wonderful things in his Book.

Notes

FOOTNOTES

1 Dallas Willard, *Renovation of the Heart: Putting on the Character of Christ* (Colorado Springs: NavPress, 2002), page 86.

2 "Did Yeshua Make Peter the Pope?" One for Israel, https://www.oneforisrael.org/bible-based-teaching-from-israel/bible-teachings/yeshua-make-peter-pope/.

3 Dickens, Charles, *A Christmas Carol* (Cambridge: Candlewick Press, 2006), page 7.

Also by CHRISTY FITZWATER

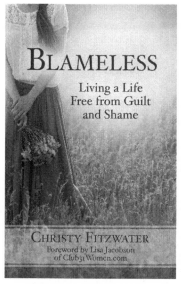

BLAMELESS

Living a Life
Free from Guilt
and Shame

CHRISTY FITZWATER
Foreword by Lisa Jacobson
of Club31Women.com

Don't you get tired of going to bed at night feeling like a failure and then waking up the next day confident that you're going to keep being a failure at just about every-thing? Add to that the feel-ing that God is waiting to smoosh you if you mess up or at least to shake his head at you in disappointment.

But it has always been God's plan for you to become blameless.

He's not waiting to hammer you if you blow it. Instead He is daily, patiently shaping you to be faultless.

It may feel too good to be true.

But what if you could believe that God is doing a great work to make you perfect, and what if you could even mark on the door frame how much taller your soul is growing every day? Wouldn't that hope change everything?

> *"I've read hundreds of books in my life, many of them very good. But few have made me laugh so much, giv-en me so much hope, and made me so eager to share its pages with my friends."* ~ Elisabeth Adams

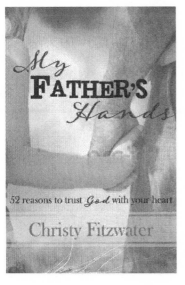

My
FATHER'S
Hands

52 reasons to trust *God* with your heart

Christy Fitzwater

You want to know God, and that requires calling him "Father". How does that make you feel? Based on your life experiences, what images come to mind with the word "father"?

This book is an invitation into my childhood home.

It's a warm and cheerful environment with a mom and dad, lots of laughter, affection, loving discipline, and just the right amount of spoiling.

Come in.

Sit down and let me fix you a cup of tea. Watch how my dad treats me as I am growing up. See the outpouring of his love. Feel how safe it is and how a girl can thrive and become someone beautiful in this kind of father-daughter relationship.

Then, with fresh perspective gained from witnessing 52 moments between my dad and me, may you feel hopeful enough to place your life in God's hands.

You can trust Him to be a good Father.

46898766R00110

Made in the USA
San Bernardino, CA
09 August 2019